THE HIDDEN WORDS OF JESUS
A Commentary on the Gospel of Thomas

THE HIDDEN WORDS OF JESUS
A Commentary on the Gospel of Thomas

George Breed

ANAMCHARA BOOKS

Copyright © 2013 by Anamchara Books, a Division of Harding House Publishing, Inc. All rights reserved. No part of this publication may be reproduced or transmitted in any form or by any means, electronic or mechanical, including photocopying, recording, taping, or any information storage and retrieval system, without permission from the publisher.

Anamchara Books
Vestal, NY 13850
www.AnamcharaBooks.com

Printed in the United States of America.

First Printing
9 8 7 6 5 4 3 2 1

IngramSpark 2020 paperback ISBN: 978-1-62524-809-1

Library of Congress Control Number: 2013933516

Our version of the Gospel of Thomas is an informal and con-versational interpretation of the Coptic text as translated by Thomas O. Lambdin, Stevan Davies, and Elaine Pagel. As much as possible, we have used non-gendered language.

Scripture quotations are from the English Revised Version of the Bible (Oxford University Press, 1885).

INTRODUCTION

An Illuminating and Mystifying Book

"These are the hidden [or secret] sayings that the living Jesus spoke and that Didymos Judas Thomas wrote down": these opening words of the Gospel of Thomas send a thrill through the heart of any reader. After 2,000 years of history influenced by Jesus of Nazareth, here is the promise of fresh words from Christ. At the same time, there's a whiff of hidden mysteries in the air. Why are these sayings "secret"? Who is Didymos Judas Thomas? Where did this book come from and why isn't it included among the Gospels in the Bible?

For a very long time, the Gospel of Thomas was truly hidden. Scholars heard rumors of its existence—several early Christian writers refer to it and one quotes from it—but the actual text was believed to be forever lost. Then, in 1945, Egyptian farmers from the village of Nag Hammadi dug up a clay jar filled with ancient books. When scholars examined these documents, they recognized a treasure trove of lost knowledge about early Christianity. The jar contained more than fifty different religious texts that differ from books handed down through Christian tradition.

The Gospel of Thomas written in Coptic (ancient Egyptian) was among the Nag Hammadi texts. After reading the Coptic version of Thomas, scholars realized they already possessed fragments of the same book written in Greek, found a half-century earlier. These Egyptian and Greek documents are the basis for the English translations of Thomas that are available today.

The writer's title describes this book as secret or hidden sayings spoken by the living Jesus. How are they "secret" and why is Jesus described as "living"? The two questions are related.

At first, scholars thought that Thomas's writings might reflect the beliefs of an early Christian sect known as Gnostics. (Gnostics held views concerning the nature of God and of Christ that differed from those in the canonical New Testament.) Since other Nag Hammadi texts contain Gnostic teaching, scholars assumed that Thomas did likewise. For the most part, however, this view has been discredited. However, while the Gospel of Thomas might not be a Gnostic book per se, it does share with the Gnostics an emphasis on mysticism—that is, the idea that Christ should be experienced directly by believers, not just encountered as an intellectual idea. Thus, the sayings in Thomas are those of the *living* Christ: not just the historical Jesus but the Spirit of Christ that speaks throughout the ages.

These sayings of Jesus are hidden in the sense that their deeper meanings are not immediately obvious. They are like the koans that Zen Buddhist masters use to coax learners into deeper, more intuitive truths. Interpretation of these sayings comes from within the hearts of believers as they commune with the living Christ.

Does this emphasis on hidden meanings and on the mystical Jesus mean that the sayings in Thomas are not those of the historical Jesus? Scholars differ in their opinions on this matter, but many believe that Thomas contains retellings of Christ's teachings similar to those in the four Christian Gospels. That is to say, the Gospel of Thomas, like the other Gospels in the Christian Bible, underwent a process that began with oral tradition and ended with a text that reflects the writer's interpretations. Likewise, Thomas and the New Testament Gospels have translated Jesus' words from the original Aramaic into Greek (and in Thomas's case, eventually into Coptic).

We cannot know for certain how many of the sayings included in the Gospel of Thomas were spoken by the historical Jesus because the existing copies of Thomas are enigmatic regarding their date and point of origin. These copies were written in the second century, but several experts believe that earlier versions of Thomas might date to a mere couple of decades after Jesus' lifetime. Half the sayings in Thomas have parallels in the New Testament Gospels, but scholars are not certain whether Matthew, Mark, Luke, and John quoted Thomas—or vice versa.

Another difficulty in pegging Thomas down to history is our uncertainty regarding the author. The first words credit Didymos Judas Thomas as the writer. Ancient Syrian tradition says this Thomas, "the twin" (Didymos), was the brother of Jesus. He is popularly known as "doubting Thomas" due to his unbelief expressed in John's Gospel. Yet scholars are uncertain that Thomas the Apostle wrote this book, just as they question whether Matthew or John wrote the books that bear their names.

And the questions continue: If this book is ancient and ascribed to an apostle, why is it not found in our Bibles today? And again, answers from scholars vary and differ from one another.

Maybe the Gospel of Thomas circulated in the wrong circles. It appears to have been favored among the Syrian Christian community. Although these were among the earliest Christians and they spoke the same Aramaic language that Jesus spoke, they nonetheless lacked influence with the authorities who defined the contents of the New Testament.

The Gospel of Thomas also suffered from association with the wrong crowd. Several Christian writers in the fourth and fifth century ascribed it to the Manichaean sect (moral dualists originating in the Persian regions where the Gospel of Thomas was popular). The text shows no evidence of Manichaean thought, but it wouldn't be the first case of exclusion due to false associations.

There's also a third view: Thomas wasn't included among the Gospels because it isn't a gospel! All the Gospels in the Bible share a common style: they interweave stories about Jesus with sayings by Jesus. The placement of teachings within a narrative framework adds important elements for the reader's understanding. Thomas, by contrast, doesn't contain any narrative about Jesus' life or actions, only direct sayings. So it is more like the Book of Proverbs in the Hebrew Bible—a collection of sayings—than it is like the Gospels. Another set of Jesus' sayings—a hypothetical collection that Bible scholars call Q—was quoted by the Gospel writers but not included in the final rendering of the Bible.

We may never be able to answer the questions posed by this enigmatic collection of Jesus' sayings, but they still offer tremendous rewards to modern readers. The living Jesus who teaches us in these texts is both familiar and fresh; his words are recognizably the same voice as Christ in the Bible, yet each saying offers perspectives that differ from the familiar texts.

One Zen Roshi of American origins has declared, "Had I known the Gospel of Thomas, I wouldn't have had to become Buddhist!" Indeed, the living Jesus in this book offers a dynamic view of life that many modern seekers find refreshing and similar to the values found in Asian religions.

More than the other Gospels, Thomas requires the reader to cooperate with the Spirit of Christ to bring forth hidden depths of meaning—and that is why George Breed is the perfect guide through this book. George is a modern mystic, a man who listens to the Presence within his own heart to interpret sacred words. The Gospel of Thomas will only yield its riches to those who walk in union with the One whose voice speaks through its pages, to those who make a determined effort to live truth as well as they learn it. We are all fortunate that George Breed has walked such a path—and now he invites us to journey along with him, guided by the hidden sayings of the living Jesus.

—*Ken McIntosh*

FOREWORD

In each of the four canonical Gospels, a story—a narrative—was woven around Jesus' sayings. With the Gospel of Thomas, we have the sayings not wrapped in a context. These sayings are understood to be in a more pure, unadulterated form, passed along through oral tradition, and eventually written down.

To understand the writings or speaking of another, we must enter that person's consciousness, adopt his mindset, look through his eyes at the world he describes, listen with his ears. Jesus often said, "Let those who have ears, hear!"

Listening requires not imposing a pre-existing dogmatic framework over what is being spoken, but allowing its imagery and meaning to unfold on its own. Rather than jumping on a sentence with analytic fervor, we allow it to settle like a depth charge—and to explode to reveal its meaning.

This is the method I followed with each saying of Jesus in writing this commentary on the Gospel of Thomas. I sat quietly in the pre-dawn hours of the night and contemplated a particular saying, allowing images and understandings to form. Eventually these imaginal formings began to solidify into sentence structures, translations from heartfelt imagery to English. I wrote each sentence as it formed. I then made small edits until I was satisfied that the sentences were as identical as possible to the images that formed from meditation on the saying. Something within "clicked" when that happened. I exhaled a sigh of completion.

Here is the outcome.

–*George Breed*

These are the hidden sayings spoken by the living Jesus and written down by Judas Thomas the Twin.

RESURRECTION

1
And he said,
"Whoever finds the meaning of these sayings
will not experience death."

To understand these sayings, our consciousness must shift. The place from which they can be understood is the place of Spirit: the eternal Life Force, That-Which-Breathes-Us, the Source that births us. To understand these sayings, we must shift our awareness to a non-death place. We drop all social roles, all social fictions, all favored illusions and preoccupations. We stand naked and empty and open.

Though our body is still here, we have already died, already "passed over." We continue surrendering, letting go. We are in the world, but not of the world. These sayings are spoken from Deep Reality. To understand them, we move into those depths. Our consciousness becomes the same Consciousness from which they are spoken. We are resurrected before we die.

As it says in the Gospel of Philip: "On the banks of the Jordan, Yeshua manifested the Presence of a realm that existed before all things."

THE DISTURBANCE OF THE SEEKER

2

Jesus said,
"Keep seeking until you find.
When you find, you will become disturbed.
After being disturbed, you will be astonished.
Then you will reign over everything."

A seeker is someone who is satisfied with neither her consciousness state nor the accepted explanations of Reality. A seeker courses beyond the surface chit-chat of human society, beyond the dogma and doctrine of nationalism, of corporatism, and other forms of religion.

A seeker finds that the outer infinity and the inner infinity are the same infinity. A seeker finds that the imaginal is real. The seeker is disturbed . . . and then astonished by finding Who is seeking.

All cognitive frames fall away and the seeker is silent, in the silence out of which all arises.

This silence reigns over everything.

THE SKY? THE SEA?
INSIDE! OUTSIDE!

3a
Jesus said, "If those who lead you say,
'Look, the Kingdom is in the sky,'
then the birds of the sky will be there ahead of you.
If they say to you, 'It is in the sea,'
then the fish will be there before you.
Rather, the Kingdom is inside you,
and it is outside you."

"Inside" is an inner infinity. When we truly know what is within us, we know a vast openness. We are not entrapped in chattering thoughts, nor are we slaves to imagery. We do not identify with the rumblings and burbling of our bodies. Thoughts, images, physical sensations, and emotions exist, but we are not attached to them. "Inside," we are infinite space and eternal time.

"The Kingdom" is the energy realm of our Source, the realm that assumes form, that is assuming the form we are now, the ever-changing form of the Formless. We belong to the Kingdom. We are manifestations of the Kingdom.

The Formless peers through our formed and forming eyes. We short-circuit it with our manufactured identities. We are a "man-you-factory." We are little gods, co-creators. We test our man-you-factorying abilities. We create some pretty weird stuff—and some wonderfulness too. The wonderfulness emerges when we create in synchrony with the Larger Flow.

The Kingdom—the Larger Flow—is both within us and outside us, an inner infinity and an outer infinity. When we let go of the carbuncular self-image we create, the two infinities easily and readily flow as one. We are a conduit of infinite Flow. We live happily and joyously in the Kingdom.

THE POVERTY
OF NOT UNDERSTANDING

3b
"When you understand yourselves,
then you will be understood,
and you will realize you are the
children of the living Father.
But if you do not know yourselves,
you exist in poverty, and you are that poverty."

We have been told elsewhere (by Socrates) that "the unexamined life is not worth living." If we stay wrapped in the cotton swathing of our being with no thought or awareness of who and what we are, of our source and destiny, our process and our flow, our enfolding and unfolding, we are an unopened package, a seed in infertile ground.

Jesus takes this insight a step further: *When you understand yourselves, then you will be understood.* A reciprocity exists: a process that happens naturally, automatically. The more room I open within my being, the greater room there is to be understood. The greater my capacity for understanding, the more I am understood.

By whom am I understood? Other people? Jesus' meaning contains that thought and much more. There is richness here, a new golden rule: "Understand yourself as you would have others understand you." But the wealth of Jesus' statement goes still deeper.

We are embodyings of the Life Force, of the energetic spirit of our Source. As we begin to know that, to consciously embody that spirit, to awaken from any illusion of separation, we create more room for the Life Force. We begin to realize, as Jesus says, that we are children *of the living Father*. And so: *When you understand yourselves, then you will be understood,* understood by the living Father, by our Source.

The greater the room of understanding we open within ourselves, the more we are understood by our Source. The greater the comprehension, the greater the Comprehension. As Meister Eckhart puts it: "The eye with which I see God is the same eye with which God sees me." This is a co-creative endeavor.

When we are full of ourselves, we cannot be understood. We talk with our spiritual mouths full, stuttering and sputtering, spraying our dry crumbs of incomprehension in all directions.

When we do not know ourselves we *exist in poverty* and *we are that poverty*. When we do not know we are children of the living Father, embodyings of our Source, we have no room in the "*In*" of ourselves, no place for the Christ Child to be born.

THE OLD MAN AND THE BABY

4a
Jesus said,
"The old man will not hesitate
to ask a seven-day-old baby
about the place of life,
and he will live."

We continue to shed the skin of an enclosed consciousness before it becomes a thick rind. We do so by continuing to allow ourselves to be open, to urge our established, settled, static selves to be receptive to the newness of existing. We see things through the eyes of the newly arrived who are still arriving. Our frozen rigidness falls away. Soft, supple, with eyes of wonder, we are alive.

A SINGLE ONE

4b
*"For many who are first will become last.
They will become a single one."*

This is not a saying about our place in society. It speaks of something much more important, of becoming "single." First is the place of the beginning. Last is the place of the end.

In saying 18, Jesus says the beginning will become the place of the end, and that anyone who stands in the beginning and knows the end will never die. This is the place of the Eternal Now. When we are fully, completely present Here, without adornment, we are forever beginning and always ending. The two are the same place. We become someone who is unified, single.

When fully present with no clinging to a past nor imagining a future, we are "in the world but not of the world." There is no first and last. We are each the same, we are all one.

NOTHING HIDDEN

5

Jesus said,
"Recognize what is right in front of you,
and that which is hidden from you
will become plain to you.
All that is hidden will be displayed."

We humans generally move through the world—exist in the Cosmos—as if it were a mere backdrop to our individual and societal melodramas: Everything centers around Me and Mine. In living this way, as inflated separate particles amid vastness, we do not recognize what is right in front of us. Much of the time, we see nothing but the movies we play in our mental theaters.

When we "come to" from our self-induced comas, when we emerge blinking from the darkened halls we thought to be reality, we begin to see what was hidden from us, what we hid from ourselves. What is right in front of us, perfectly visible, is what we couldn't see. It is what we were looking for in our theatrical plots and scenes. What was outside is now inside, and we see that the outside and the inside are the same. The Face of the Cosmos is staring us in the face—and the Eye with which it gazes and our eyes are the same Eye.

Nothing is hidden anymore, for there is no place of separation for hiding.

THE INSUFFICIENCY OF A MORAL CODE

6

His disciples questioned him,
"Do you want us to fast?
How shall we pray?
Shall we give to the poor?
What diet shall we observe?"
Jesus answered,
"Do not lie,
and do not do what you hate,
for all things are revealed beneath heaven.
Everything hidden will be revealed,
and everything covered will be disclosed."

Those whom Jesus taught, those of the inner circle who stayed with him as much as possible, looked for guidance on specific questions. Presented here is a set of three, all three having to do with correct religious or spiritual practice: *Do you want us to fast? How shall we pray? Shall we give to the poor?* The disciples know from experience that Jesus is an iconoclastic teacher. He blows apart conventional teachings to reveal their inner core of meaning. Fasting was an accepted way of cleansing yourself from impurity. Praying was setting up a link between yourself and the Divine. Giving to charity was one way to perform good deeds, healing actions in society. Where, the disciples wonder, does Jesus stand on these three? In this saying, Jesus responds obliquely. He gives a more direct response in saying 14a: *If you fast, you will bring sin to yourselves; and if you pray, you will be condemned; and if you give to charity, you will harm your spirits.*

Oh boy. Here we go again. Jesus gives unexpected replies contradictory to the usual teachings in these matters. If you do these three things, you will bring sin to yourself, be condemned, and harm your spirit. How can this be?

When you are born again of the Spirit, as Jesus advocated, each of these three is a step backward to your previous state of consciousness. Fasting, praying, and giving are techniques, methods, and practices of the once-born; they are designed for two things: to live a good moral life and to serve as a platform for consciousness change. Once this consciousness change occurs and you open to the Life Flow of Spirit, getting stuck in those three practices as your religion—allowing them to define the boundaries of your connection to God—will damage your spirit.

This phrase—being born again—which has been subject to much ridicule and misunderstanding, means you have dropped the world of form as your anchor point; you have opened yourself to living in the Tao—the Life Force, the Flow of the Source, the Wellspring—*as* the Tao. You live in the world of form as the formless. In this second birthing, this evolution of consciousness, you follow the flow of Spirit, of the Life Force. (Lao Tzu put it this way: *Those who flow as life flows know they need no other force. They feel no wear, they feel no tear. They need no mending, no repair.*) In doing so, if we lie, it will throw us out of the Flow. If we do what we hate, we will separate ourselves from the Truth. As soon as we deviate from the Path (call it what you will: the Way, the Tao, the Flow), our misstep will be immediately obvious. We know when we are running into the ditch.

THAT LION
WILL BECOME HUMAN

7
Jesus said,
"Blessed is the lion that a person eats,
because that lion will become human;
and cursed is the person whom the lion eats,
for that lion will become human."

We have a blessing and a curse here, a blessed action and a cursed action, with what seems to be the same result: a lion becomes human. The first action is that the human eats the lion. The second action is that the lion eats the human. Since in both cases the lion becomes human, the focus must be on the way the lion becomes human.

The First Epistle of Peter (5:8) says the devil walks about like a roaring lion seeking whom he may devour. When we think of the lion in this manner, we can see why the person the lion eats would be cursed: the person has been eaten by the devil.

Now what does that mean: to be eaten—to be swallowed whole—by the devil? In this enlightened age, people do not believe in the devil, and yet, I assure you, the devil exists. The devil is that part of you that wishes to rebel—and does rebel—against love and understanding, against compassion and wisdom. The two interflow, you know. When compassionate, we are wise. When wise, we are compassionate. Intellect in the service of love is wise.

When devoured by the lion, however, we are unloving and unwise. We sit in the lion's belly, consumed by its three digestive juices: greed, hostility, and stupor. Greed is wanting what we do not have. Hostility is not wanting what we *do* have. Stupor is just plain ignore-ance, not letting ourselves be aware of our true situation: that we are in the belly of the lion.

Cursed is the person whom the lion eats, for that lion will become human. When the lion devours us, we are all of us—whoever we are—greedy, hostile, and ignorant. This result spans nationalities. It crosses religious boundaries. The lion recognizes no such lines of demarcation.

But we haven't looked yet at the first way that the lion can become human. Jesus calls it the blessed or blessing way. We do not cast the lion from us. That is a grievous error and an illusion. The lion is part of us. We own it. We own our greed, our hostility, our stupor. In owning it, we swallow it whole. We have met the lion and the lion is us (to paraphrase the immortal Pogo). The human devours the lion, eats him alive. A human cannot do this alone. But we are not alone. There are powerful spiritual forces, which make up one Force, with whom we can ally. Then we can eat the lion.

Now the lion has become human in a different way. We have consumed the lion. It is part of our own hearts, and now we have a certain fierceness: a fiercely compassionate wisdom.

What a blessing!

THE FINE LARGE FISH
OF BENEFIT

8
And he said,
"The Kingdom is like a wise fisherman
who cast his net into the sea
and drew it up from the sea full of small fish.
Among them the wise fisherman found a fine large fish.
He threw all the small fish back into the sea
and without hesitation chose the large one.
Whoever has ears to hear, hear this!"

We are not called only to be fishermen—people who seek treasure out of the Great Ocean—but wise fishermen. We must have some degree of insight or wisdom, as well as a relentless steadfastness (one aspect of wisdom) that allows us to experience all the small fish until we find the fine large fish. To do this, we will have already moved past the foam, the flotsam and jetsam of superficiality, casting our nets deep into the sea again and again, until the fine large fish is caught, the one that will benefit us most.

What is this fish but our very own souls? We have caught the true beings we are. Nothing else is of benefit to us but that energetic Flow of our own selves, which comes from and is the Great Ocean Itself. If we can hear the Ocean, we know this as truth.

GOOD SOIL

9
Jesus said,
"Look, a sower went out,
took a handful of seeds, and scattered them.
Some fell on the road, and the birds ate them.
Others fell on the rock,
did not take root, and did not grow.
And others fell on thorns;
the thorns choked them, and worms consumed them.
And others fell on good ground
and produced good fruit:
they bore 60 per measure and 120 per measure."

We hear and see according to our capacity. The seed is the wisdom of the universe, the wisdom of the Cosmos, of God: the knowing and understanding that surpasses all worldly education.

We do not receive this wisdom if we are a well-trodden road of surface routine. Instead, we will dismiss this wisdom as soon as it lands on our consciousness. Nor can these seeds of understanding who and what we are—of opening to the energies that birth this world—find any place to root if our heart-mind is rock or if our thoughts are prickly and thorny. Self-reflective thought is hard ground. A mirror has no place for seed; it has no place for anything but what it reflects. When focusing on me, me, me, my soil is hard and slick. Nothing worthy can get in.

In the physical world, humus is good soil. In the spiritual realm, *humus* translates into "humble," into "humility." To receive increased understanding, we must become the dirt we are. Surrender is a word we all detest, yet surrender is exactly what is needed.

THE FIRE
OF TRANSFORMATION

10
Jesus said,
"I have thrown fire on the world.
Look! I am guarding it until it blazes."

The world was destroyed by water once. Next time, said the prophecy, will be the fire. That time is now. The fire is here. A great consciousness change is underway. Fire has been cast upon the world.

The world (human society) is a direct outgrowth of human consciousness. The current world, upon which fire has been cast, is one largely produced by divisive consciousness.

And what is this next form of consciousness arising but the Fire itself? The Fire of elation, of coming home, of being at home in the universe.

Jesus came as an advance rep of this fiery consciousness. That is why his head is shown ablaze in all those halo paintings.

Divisiveness is dissolving; it is set ablaze. Unitive consciousness is evolving and with it a new epoch in the human journey.

Look to the fire within you. Tend it until it blazes.

Jesus has thrown his fire on the world!

SKY

11a
Jesus said,
"The sky will pass away,
and the sky above it will pass away as well."

"The sky's the limit."

We see no farther than the sky in our ordinary consciousness, even though there is a sky beyond that. This first sky, this here-and-now realm—this limited ordinary consciousness—can cease to be even now. This is part of what is meant by "dying before you die." Do we ever consider ordinary consciousness to be death? And that dying to ordinary consciousness is life? When we see beyond this first sky, we will be no longer entrapped by it.

The sky above it, which will also cease to be, is the limitation of our spiritual insight. When we reach that place, all bounds are removed, and our spiritual insight is unlimited, ever increasing. We will know no bounds; we will be boundless. We will be part of a circle with no circumference, a sphere with no surface.

Can we handle that? Or will we cling to our tight little virginal consciousness?

THE DEAD AND THE LIVING

11b
"The dead do not live,
and the living will not die."

While living only to satisfy the body, we are spiritually dead. Our consciousness is creature consciousness. When we do not live in accord with the Flow of the Life Force that is forever birthing us, we are dead to the energy of the Cosmos. We feel a sense of separation that puffs and snorts with disconsolate emotion and false inflation.

Those who recognize their identity with this eternal birthing, however, never die. They are the embodying of the Life Force, of the out-breathing of the Spirit that never dies. The deep awareness of this is the second and true birth.

ARRIVAL

11c
*"When you ate dead things, you made them alive.
When you come to dwell in the light, what will you do?"*

A shifting of gears occurs here, a transformation across three realms. Each transformation feeds off the one before.

First is the physical, the eating of dead things. (We would rather call them food.) We humans are scavengers, though we are particular in our scavenging, preferring to eat the newly dead. Jesus says that in doing so, we make the dead alive: the things we eat walk around as us. This is the second of the first two realms. The third realm is light.

What is going to happen when we arrive into light? What will we do? Though we may gripe and complain, we cling to being human. We do not wish to be dead meat. We want to keep driving in second gear.

Too bad. Jesus says we are going to shift into third: we will come to dwell in the light. What will we do then? Just as the dead becomes us when we eat it, so we become the light when it devours us whole.

There go all our plans.

MULTIPLE PERSONALITY DISORDER

11d

*"When you were one, you became two.
But when you become two,
what will you do?"*

We suffer from multiple personality disorder—every one of us. We were each conceived as one, as a oneness. We floated in amniotic fluid with every wish fulfilled instantly. Then we entered the world of differentiation, of discrimination. We each became two.

Though it may seem as if the entire galloping horde of our many selves descends upon us at once, we really deal with only two at a time: this and that, here and there, me and you, us and them. We are no longer unified. We have even divided the world into the spiritual and the physical. No separation exists, but we have made it so.

What will we do now that we have each become two? When a person is two, she is quite insane. This split is evident in the civilization we have built, one that is unsustainable.

The answer to Jesus' question is simple. We can "let the light of our eye be single," opening to the awareness that we are inseparable from the Interflow, from the vast interconnecting and ever-changing Sphere of Being (a sphere with no bounds). In that case, we are always already home, safe, sound, secure, ever-changing, and adventuring.

Or we can continue birthing our own insanity.

What will you do?

JAMES THE JUST

12
His disciples said to Jesus,
"We know you will leave us.
Who will be our leader?"
Jesus answered,
"Wherever you are, go to James the Just,
for whose sake heaven and earth came into being."

Humans need a physical leader, someone embodied in the flesh, who shares their worldly situation. When Jesus was physically gone, what were his followers, his students, to do? Who could ever take the place of Jesus?

Jesus has a ready answer. He does not speak here of the forthcoming Holy Spirit, the Paraclete, as the disciples' inner guide. He does not foretell the leadership of Paul, a latecomer to the movement. Instead, he names his brother James, whose spirit was evidently in tune with Jesus' spirit ("for whose sake heaven and earth came into being").

Apparently, James led very well. His ongoing capability as a leader was acknowledged and certified by his becoming the first bishop of Jerusalem.

THE BUBBLING SPRING

13a
Jesus said to his disciples,
"Compare me to someone
and tell me whom I am like."
Simon Peter said to him,
"You're like a righteous messenger."
Matthew said to him,
"You're like a wise philosopher."
Thomas said to him,
"Master, my mouth is wholly incapable
of saying whom you are like."
Jesus said,
"I am not your master.
Because you have drunk,
you have become intoxicated
by the bubbling spring I have poured out."

Jesus' framing of his question is important. He does not ask: "Who am I?" That would be too vague and peculiar a question. He understands that we think in metaphors and comparisons, so he says: *Compare me to someone and tell me whom I am like.*

Peter's answer—*You are like a righteous messenger*—sounds good at first glance, but it is somewhat distancing, putting Jesus over there somewhere, someone from somewhere else who has come to set things straight. It implies that Peter was ready to join the movement and set a few things straight himself.

Matthew's answer—*You are like a wise philosopher*—makes Jesus a little more human, but it is distancing too. As a lover (philo) of wisdom (sopher), Jesus would be in a category of people of intelligent abstraction.

Thomas says, in effect, "Master, I cannot possibly say what you are like." In his answer, Thomas acknowledges Jesus as his *sensei*, his teacher; and in the best Zen tradition, Thomas says he has no words to describe Jesus—none will fit.

Jesus totally ignores the answers of Peter and Matthew. He goes to the answer that has some life in it. First of all, though, he has to set Thomas straight: *I am not your master.* With those words, Jesus abolishes the hierarchy. He speaks the truth of equality in the capacity for understanding. He knows that Thomas has great capaciousness. He also knows that Thomas's ordinary consciousness is reeling from the wisdom and understanding that is flowing in. Jesus says Thomas is intoxicated from the bubbling water of wisdom that Jesus has been pouring out.

Jesus not only poured out effervescent wisdom with his verbal words, but also—and probably even more so—with the radiance of his presence, with his nonverbal outspokenness. Thomas feels this; his consciousness is resonant with Jesus' consciousness. He vibrates with it. He is spiritually drunk.

Jesus knows this and takes Thomas aside from the others to tell him a few things. About that, we'll hear more later, in the second part of saying 13.

THOMAS WITHDRAWS WITH JESUS AND RETURNS

13b
*And he took him and withdrew
and told him three things.
When Thomas returned to his companions,
they asked him, "What did Jesus say to you?"
Thomas said to them,
"If I tell you one of the things he told me,
you will pick up stones and throw them at me,
and fire will come out of the stones and burn you up."*

On another occasion, Jesus cautioned his followers not to throw their pearls into the hog pen. We can only receive wisdom and understanding according to our capacity, our emptiness. When we are full of ourselves, we cannot hear; when our minds are made up like a bed in the morning, new ideas cannot slide beneath the covers. If we have ideas about who

Jesus is and what he is like, he can stand right in front of us and tell us differently—and we will not hear him. We may even condemn him for blasphemy.

Peter and Matthew have their minds made up, while Thomas is open and receptive. Jesus calls him aside, away from the others. (Our quiet time alone and open, away from "the maddening crowd," is essential for our spiritual growth and discernment. "Closet yourself and pray," said Jesus.)

Jesus tells Thomas three things. What they are is not as important as that they are told. They are three specific communications from a person of cosmic awareness that the ordinary (ordinal) mind would not comprehend. But Thomas is ready to hear them. Afterward, Thomas does not go off into his own personal nirvana and remain isolated from humankind. He follows the path of the bodhisattva and returns "to the marketplace."

The rest of the group is of course dying with anticipation: "What did he tell you? What did he tell you?" Thomas follows the example of Jesus and keeps his mouth shut. Some of the things we are told in private, in prayer and meditation and contemplation, are to be kept to ourselves. They are to sit within us and continue to generate spiritual energy and understanding. If we speak them aloud, they lose some of their sacredness. Especially if we speak to someone who does not comprehend.

Thomas tells them: *If I tell you one of the sayings he told me, you will pick up stones and throw them at me.* In other words, they would be shocked out of their gourds. Those who were considered blasphemous were stoned in those days. (These days it is much easier to color outside the orthodox lines. It is expected, even longed for sometimes. The old shoes are way too tight.)

Thomas does not stop there. He continues: *and fire will come out of the stones and burn you up*. There. That tells us a little about what Thomas was told. He has begun to learn about the nature of the universe. The stone you throw at another destroys yourself.

MOVING PAST ASCETICISM

14a
Jesus said to them,
"If you fast, you will bring sin to yourselves;
and if you pray, you will be condemned;
and if you give to charity, you will harm your spirits."

Jesus' sayings often directly contradict orthodox Christianity. This is because he is speaking in the realm of spirit and not the flesh. On other occasions, he speaks of resurrecting before you die, of being born not just of water (amniotic fluid) but of spirit: the second birth. The rules of the amnion do not apply to one born in the aeon. Jesus often broke the amnion world's rules.

When we are already born into the Kingdom—when we are Kingdom residents, spirits in the realm of Spirit, energy-beings amid Energy—to focus on fasting, praying, and giving to charity would be like crawling on our hands and knees once we've learned to walk. Those three, in the sense used here, are the flesh-denying steps we take in order to learn to function in the realm of the spirit. The skills we learned on our hands and knees are incorporated into our walking—but we need no longer practice those skills, for we have internalized them.

As Mister Buddha said, once you reach the other shore, you don't carry your boat around on your head.

WALKING AROUND IN EVERYDAY LIFE AS A HEALER

14b
*"When you go into any land
and walk from place to place,
whenever people receive you,
eat what they set before you,
and heal their sick."*

Jesus was a Teacher. Here, he is instructing his pupils in the spiritual pathways and an appropriate procedure to follow when they go into a region. Jesus' words reflect his own approach to life. He hung out with the everyday folk, the outcasts, the poor, and the renegades. He did not drive the latest chariot or dine in the fanciest places. He did not even drive an oxcart. He walked. In this way, he easily met people; he was easily approachable. Here he is instructing his students to do the same.

When you go into any land and walk from place to place, whenever people receive you... When you are out there walking around (not knocking on doors), people will make eye contact or say hello. This is being received. Or people may ask you to sit down for a moment or to walk alongside them; they may invite you into their homes. This is being received.

. . .*whenever people receive you, eat what they set before you.* When you meet people, they always have something with which they are dealing, something they are trying to work out, something they have yet to resolve. Jesus says to his pupils, "Eat that. Do not stand there talking about yourself. Open yourself to the other. Listen."

. . .*what* THEY *set before for you.* A person will disclose as much as she is willing to disclose, whatever is comfortable to disclose. This is a natural process. Don't reach your hand of inquiry into the other person's mouth, down into his gullet, grab hold, and turn him inside out. If you are fully present, without any agenda except to be in the unfolding interpersonal interplay, the other person's speaking and your own listening become a seamless flow.

. . .*eat what they set before you, and heal their sick.* Listen to—eat—whatever they set before you, and in so doing, a healing process will be underway. All sickness is imbalance. To heal means "to make whole," "to bring into balance." Healing is not one person doing something to another person. Healing is a dynamic dance, an energetic merge. Both people are doing the dance. This is not power over another person. This is power with each other. Healing takes place in all realms: physical, mental, emotional, interpersonal, societal. All is made whole; all is made holy.

INTAKE AND OUTFLOW

14c
"For what goes into your mouth will not defile you, but that which comes out of your mouth —that is what will defile you."

With the right spirit, we can take in anything we run into and it will not defile us; it will not poison our inner beings, our spirits. Jesus took in all the rottenness of humankind and devilish forces. Buddha took in all that Mara had to throw at him. It didn't hurt either one of them a bit. They stayed right where they were, unmoved: Jesus on the cross tree, Buddha beneath the bodhi tree.

What comes out of the mouth of our beings is what can defile us, not what goes in. And it does not even have to be spoken aloud. The smallest thought can dislodge us. As the I Ching says, "If you are off by a hair's breadth at the beginning, you will miss by a thousand miles at the end."

Take it all in and let it all go. This is breathing in and breathing out. No clinging. No impediments. In-hale. (*Hale* means healthy.) Ex-hale. Breathe in healthiness. Breathe out healthiness.

If we are strong enough, we can breathe in the hell around us, slurping it up like a cosmic vacuum cleaner. In-hell (like Jesus and Buddha).

But for goodness sake, do not ex-hell! Breathe out a clear, positive, loving spirit to all around.

THE BORN
AND THE UNBORN

15
Jesus said,
"When you see someone
who was not born of woman,
prostrate yourselves and worship.
That one is your Father."

The surface part of ourselves, the part that makes contact with the world and in some sense is the world, is the aspect of ourselves "born of woman." This is the character, the personality we are, the persona that builds, that accretes, ever since physical birth. This is the froth on the wave of the ocean.

We can look inside and see someone not born of woman—the energetic and energizing flow of the Wellspring Itself. This is our Source, our Father. The woman-born flatlines (prostrates itself) at such a sight. The woman-born (born of water, the amniotic fluid) gives way to the spirit-born, the Life-Force–born.

We are born again. Both births are essential—of the Essence—but the new birth is the Unborn borning.

THE THROWER
OF FIRE

16a
Jesus said,
"People think, perhaps,
that I have come to cast peace upon the earth.
They do not know that it is dissension
that I have come to throw upon the world:
fire, sword, and war."

Let us look at this as a saying of Jesus the man, and then as a saying of Jesus the prophet.

As a man, Jesus knows that he is outside the mindset of the people of his day—the Romans, the Jews, the Zealots, the doctors of learning, the Samaritans, the merchants, the priests, the military, the fishermen and farmers, his family. He knows that the collision of his mindset with their mindsets will bring fierce disagreements: "fire, sword, and war." He knows that the world is ruled by mindsets—and that his mindset, if accepted, will blow the world apart. Therefore, the people who run into it have to vigorously discount it. Jesus speaks and lives his mindset anyway.

When we see Jesus as a prophet, we see his words are equally true for the events up through today. Political and religious institutions steeped in blood were built on his name. The Judeo-Christian-Muslim triumvirate—each with a different view of Jesus—mistrust each other and war with each other. About 38,000 Christian denominations exist now, each with a different mindset about Jesus.

No Prince of Peace here. No sheep-like Jesus led to the slaughter. This is Jesus the thrower of disagreement, the Thrower of Fire.

THREE AGAINST TWO AGAINST THREE

16b
"For there will be five in a house;
three will be against two,
and two against three;
father against son,
and son against father.
And they will each stand up and be alone."

The choosing of an odd number here is purposeful and pertinent. Opposition is rarely an even split. We either side with a majority or a minority. This is also true for internal transformation. To stay the same, we follow the majority vote we have always followed. Transformation requires joining the minority forces and making them the majority.

The father (that which was previously established) of our self is opposed to the son (the new awakening) of our self, and the son is opposed to the father. The father births the son who becomes the new father, and on it goes. Opposition melds into the awareness that there is nothing to oppose. The non-dual transcends. We each stand as who we are, each of us alone, a singular, solitary being. The light of our eyes is now single.

I WILL GIVE YOU THAT

17

Jesus said,
"I will give you what no eye has seen
no ear has heard, no hand has touched,
and no human mind has ever thought."

Hah! Who does Jesus think he is? Are we not already the masters of the universe? Pah! Our five senses and the thinking, rational mind are plenty enough, thank you! Do we not already have philosophers so profound that only a few people understand what those thinkers are saying? Haven't we invented machines that suck the Earth dry of the resources we need to maintain ourselves in the luxury to which we have grown accustomed? Shall we not eventually put a Coca-Cola sign on the moon? Are we not the most magnificent species ever existing? Who needs these mystical voices from beyond, claiming to know, to have an intimate connection with the source of all being? Poppycock! We are "the masters of our fate, the captains of our soul"! We need no such dreamers. We roll over Jesus' voice with our techno-war machines, spit in his face with laughing scorn, and pass him by. Jesus' consciousness is evolution gone astray. The sooner we rid the planet of his followers the better!

By the way, didn't we kill this guy off about 2,000 years ago? Why does he keep popping back up? A world beyond the one we do not recognize? No! Couldn't be! Even if there was, we would bring it under our domination and use it to further our unceasing advancement. Come to think of it, isn't our Defense Department already doing that?

Jesus wept.

Jesus is speaking of Vision, of the ability to see spiritually, of spiritual sight. With Vision, when we look at the Earth, we see not a mass to be plundered, not a yolk sac to be sucked dry so the peep of humanity can be born. We see our mother. We see a living breathing being.

With Vision, we are aware of the consciousness that is the universe. Our world shifts from the prosaic, from a bottom line to be constantly calculated, to the poetry of that which births us, that which is in constant communion with us, that which nurtures us, challenges us, brings us into fleshly existence . . . and out again.

We no longer confine ourselves to the cold eye of intellect and the desirous eye of the body. The eye of active imagination—the imaginal—bridges the two. Make no mistake: the imaginal is not the same as the imaginary. We have degraded this gift, spurned it, relegated it to scornful fantasy. We have forgotten that we are Magi, the poet-warriors of the I-magi-nal.

Crippled mewlings crawling on Earth's surface with fantasies of domination, fears of annihilation, and credit cards long gone dry, we must reclaim our vision. We must open our third eye, the eye of Spirit, of the Life Force, the eye that sees the beauty and harmony of the Cosmos.

STANDING UP
IN THE BEGINNING

18
The disciples said to Jesus,
"Tell us about our end."
Jesus said,
"Have you found the beginning,
that you're looking now for the end?
The place of the beginning is the place of the end.
Blessed is the one who stands at the beginning.
That one will know the end and never die."

The disciples want to turn to the end of the book and know the final outcome. Never mind all that stuff between now and then. Their question indicates they are having some alone time with Jesus, and now, in their minds, they can get right down to the good stuff.

They were not all that different from us these days. Never mind the here-and-now—what's going to happen later?

Jesus immediately shifts attention to the beginning. I can imagine some of the disciples thinking: *O God! Here we go again! Never a straight answer.* But Jesus is wise. He knows that straight answers result in a rigid orthodoxy of the mind.

Have you found the beginning, that you're looking now for the end? First things first. The beginning is the first of all. Do you know the beginning? Do you know the place where things spring forth? That is also the place of the end. *The place of the beginning is the place of the end.*

The beginning is where we are right now. We are always here at the beginning, where everything has its start. All creation flows out of NOW. No other place exists but Now. Everything is beginning now, while at the same time it is ending now. The beginning and the ending interflow, allowing an ongoing cycle of change.

We constantly live in a continuous flow of ending-beginning-ending-beginning. We ourselves are always ending-beginning-ending-beginning. The chopping up of this process into discrete parts is a function of our rational minds, wonderful apparatuses that often mistake their own apparitions for reality.

We live in the beginning-ending. More accurately, we are the beginning-ending. When we truly know this and are this, something amazing happens.

Blessed is the one who stands at the beginning. That one will know the end and never die. When we stand in this beginning, this Now, we know the end. When we take our place in this beginning, there is no end. When we take our place in this beginning, there is no death. Taking our place in this beginning, we never die.

BLESSED

19a
Jesus said,
"Blessed is the one who came into being
before coming into being."

Now sit with that saying for a while and see what it does to your mind! The logical-rational-deducing mind will quickly spin itself into such a state that even Cogno-WD-40 won't rescue it . . . so it'll denounce the saying as nonsense and turn its capabilities to more graspable Wal-Mart–world practicalities.

Blessed is the one who came into being before coming into being. Many of us walk around entranced as if the "names" we have been given are who we are. We act as though the birth names to which we respond define our identities. We behave as though we are nothing more than the conglomerate of expectations surrounding our names, the reputations we have carefully (and not so carefully!) produced. (Jesus deliberately "made himself of no reputation"—though we built a bunch of expectations on top of him.)

We will do everything in our power to preserve our make-believe phenomena and swear by the social contract we have all put into place to not pierce each other's phantom veils. We are real, by Zeus and Hecate! And we have the documentation to prove it!

Jesus says that blessed—happy—are you if you know you existed before you came into being. We are embodying for a while in these particular forms. We know this at a deep level but we get so caught up—so invested in our melodramas and soap operas—that we wound, kill, and die for them. No blessedness there.

(And don't go romping off into some rap that you were a pharaoh or an orphic seductress or a grand wizard in your previous lives either. That kind of thinking just means you're still caught in dreaming the ego's dreams.)

Blessed is the one who came into being before coming into being. That blessedness is plenty enough.

THESE STONES
WILL SERVE YOU

19b
*"If you become my disciples and listen to my words,
these stones will serve you."*

When we read this saying, our eyes automatically go to "stone," the weightiest part of the sentence. The eye, like water, seeks its own level.

The true weight, however, is in the initial, conditional clause, the *if* part of this if-then sentence. *If you become my disciples*: if you open yourself to my discipline (not the punishment-type of discipline; discipline like a field of study). "If you open yourself to my field of study, the realm of the God-human, the sphere of theophany, and listen to me, allow me to teach you, these stones will serve you."

They will not get up and serve us tea on a tray. They will not fly through the air and obey our commands. They will serve us by disclosing themselves to us. By opening our consciousness to knowing what they truly are. Light. Forms of light. As much a part of God's exuberance as rainbows, humming birds, humans.

Let the world reveal itself to you, rather than impose yourself upon the world. The lover senses every nuance of the beloved. Any other way is rape. Forcing our wills upon the world wounds the world, wounds the soul.

Humans are sub-human if they have no understanding of the energetic consciousness of rocks. Without such awareness, a human lives in a disenchanted universe; she is a pre-human or a facsimile human. But if we follow Jesus' discipline—his field of study—our awareness opens to the true nature of stones and the entire universe. This is a service.

Then we will find that the universe is one of mutual disclosure. We are enrolled in Theophany 101, and we are opening to Perichoresis 102. The world reveals itself to us as we follow the discipline . . . as we are Jesus' disciples.

IN
PARADISE

19c

"Five trees grow for you in Paradise;
they remain undisturbed summer and winter,
and their leaves do not fall.
Whoever comes to know them
will not taste death."

Trees are webs of energy flow, energetic systems connecting one realm with another. Here we have five trees that are eternal. Their leaves never fall. Jesus says when we come to know those trees, we will not die.

The five trees are the Tree of the Above, the Tree of the Below, the Tree of the Within, the Tree of the Without, and the Heart Tree. Together they form a dimensional cross: the Above and Below, the Internal and the External, and the Heart at the joining center.

The Tree of the Above is the glory and splendor, unending, of the Great Mystery, our Father beyond all name. The Tree of the Below is the depth and ground, falling away into infinity, of our Mother who bears us and births us without end.

The Tree of the Without is the tree of all manifestation, all that is called into Being. The Tree of the Within is the invisible and infinite Spirit, the Life Force, that vibrates its correlates Without.

The Heart Tree is the vibrant dynamic location where all Trees join. We open our Heart and all five Trees are radiant with Life. This is paradise. This is bliss.

A SHELTER
FOR THE BIRDS
OF HEAVEN

20
The disciples said to Jesus,
"Tell us what the Kingdom of Heaven is like."
He answered,
"It is like a mustard seed, the smallest of all seeds.
But when it falls on tilled soil,
it produces a large plant
and shelters the birds of heaven."

"We understand what the kingdom of earth is like. Tell us about the kingdom of heaven." All Zen masters are asked this question. What is nirvana like? What is enlightenment?

Jesus certainly does not give the answer we often imagine: harp-strumming on clouds and everything a continuous virginal pie. If any of the disciples have any thoughts in that direction, they're slammed back down into the ground of Now.

A mustard seed? The Kingdom of Heaven, such a mighty concept that it needs capitalization, is like the smallest, most overlooked of all things?

But wait! There's more! It has to fall onto worked ground before it can open to the heavenly.

Jesus is pointing to our consciousness. The Kingdom of Heaven is our consciousness, our consciousness when it remains attuned to the mystery of the smallest of things. When our consciousness falls into the tilled ground (soil from which all concrete and manufactured asphalt has been removed, so that the humus lies fallow and open), our consciousness immediately becomes a shelter for the birds of the sky.

You are a tree of life whose roots go deep into the dark, whose branches and leaves open to the light of comprehension. This is your consciousness. This is the Kingdom of Heaven.

PLAYING
IN THE FIELD

21a
Mary asked Jesus,
"What are your disciples like?"
He said,
"They are like little children
in a field that is not theirs.
When the owners of the field come, they will say,
'Give us back our field.'
They will strip naked in the owner's presence
and give their field back."

One of the Marys (perhaps his mother, perhaps Mary Magdalene) was curious about how Jesus saw his disciples, that assortment of personalities who stayed with him as much as possible and listened to his teachings. Jesus' answer shows once again that he is a visionary, that he sees with eyes of fire and light, rather than eyes of flesh.

They are like little children in a field that is not theirs. The world-field, the human societal structure that attempts to stand alone in what is perceived as an alien cosmos, is an energy field that does not belong to those who have gone past its consciousness state. What is born out of the world-field no longer belongs to it nor it to them.

At all times, the field's owners—those who have a strong investment in the field—demand their pound of flesh: *Give us back our field*. Jesus' answer to this is consistent: "Let them have the dang thing. If they ask for your coat, give them your cloak too. Give to Caesar what is Caesar's. Stand naked in the universe and rejoice."

Impractical and foolish? If you are standing in the world-field, claiming ownership of it, then, yes. If you are standing in the Tao field, the energy field of the Way, of the Cosmos and of the heavens, no. As the Zen folk put it: "No clinging. Let it all go." As Mister Bob Dylan sings: "When you got nothing, you got nothing to lose." No fear exists anymore. The world-field has no power over you.

ENERGY VAMPIRES

21b
"Therefore I say,
if the owner of a house knows a thief is coming,
he will keep watch
and will not let him break into his house
to steal his goods.
You, then, be on your guard against the world.
Arm yourselves with power,
so the robbers cannot find a way to come to you."

Energy vampires exist. They exist in both human and in non-visible form. Spiritual energy can be sucked from you: your goods stolen. Keep watch and know when this is about to happen. Notice when it is already happening.

An energy vampire will often come in a benign form in order to get close to us. What seems a natural progression ends in our depletion. We are sucked dry, left with a wounded feeling of discomfort and shock.

Rouse your awareness of the situation and "arm yourselves with power." Settle into your spiritual core. Don't let it happen.

THE EXPECTED SITUATION

21c
"The difficulty that you expect will surely materialize. Let there be with you a person of understanding."

No matter how optimistic we are, deep inside we expect that everything we have will be taken from us. This expectation is reality. All that we cling to will be removed, revealing all that we are: our essence.

At this time of no escape and no hiding place, let someone who has already been through this be with you. Such company is available on the invisible spiritual plane as well, the site where this vulnerable nakedness occurs. That person who understands is the person you continue to cultivate, to be open to: the person you are becoming. That person is the Angel of your Being.

Beware! Angels are not cute little cuddly things. When the Angel of your Being is with you, the Sword of the Spirit (the Life Force) cuts through all expectation, all sham.

THE HARVESTING OF AWARENESS

21d
"When the grain ripened,
he came quickly with his sickle
and harvested it.
Whoever has ears to hear, hear!"

As our consciousness begins to mature—to open, like a mature flower—an answering response comes from our Source. The response is quick, immediate. Our expansion of awareness is not wasted but is harvested, received with great joy.

Our awareness is matched in kind. As our capacity to understand (our ears) expands, we are given more capacity. We can hear more. This process is unending.

Attention is our tool and method. When we attend to something, we become like that thing. As our attention turns to our Source, we become more and more like our Source.

JESUS
AND THE GATELESS GATE

22

Jesus saw babies beings suckled.
He said to his disciples,
"These babies are like
those who enter the Kingdom."
His disciples asked him,
"If we are infants, will we enter the Kingdom?"
Jesus answered,
"When you make the two into one,
and when you make the inside like the outside
and the outside like the inside,
and the above like the below,
and when you make the male and the female
one and the same,
so that the male is no longer male
nor the female female;

and when you fashion eyes in the place of an eye,
and a hand in place of a hand,
and a foot in place of a foot,
and an image in place of an image,
then you will enter the Kingdom."

Jesus is a master teacher. He teaches deep truths by pointing to familiar events in daily life. His goal is to help those who are willing to move out of ordinary consciousness into a wider, deeper, boundless awareness. Using a metaphor familiar to all, he calls this awareness the Kingdom.

These babies are like those who enter the Kingdom. Complete trust, relaxation, and surrender—while maintaining individuality—the seeking and receiving nourishment from the One-Who-Breathes-Us: this is the way we enter the Kingdom.

But we do not become infants to enter the Kingdom. We become not-two. We go through a body transplant. The physical body is a seed planted in the Ground of Existence. Like all seeds it will die. The question is—the adventure is!—will it bear fruit before (or as) it dies? Entering the Kingdom is a dying to the seed-world (ordinary consciousness) and an opening to the deep grounding and expansive awareness of the non-dual world.

When you make the two into one. When we allow our consciousness state to move away from the dualistic thinking of me-you, us-them, on-the-one-hand–on-the-other-hand, when we become the hyphen separating these and all dualistic splits, and then, when even the hyphen disappears . . . then all the dualities by which ordinary consciousness is framed and deluded are released: inner-outer, upper-lower, male-female. (This is the "Gateless Gate" of Zen.) We live in infinite space and we have no gender. Our spiritual eyes have replaced our physical eyes, our seed eyes. We take on a cosmic body. We continue to act, see, and move; but now with a different hand, eye, and foot. Our whole image of who and where we are is replaced by a more astounding vision. We have entered the Kingdom.

ALONE

23

*Jesus said,
"I shall choose one of you out of a thousand,
and two of you out of ten thousand.
Those I choose will stand up and be alone."*

A teacher can only teach those whose attention is focused on learning. Those whose attention is caught in ordinary consciousness, firmly embedded in societal reality—in the mass hypnosis of their culture—cannot hear or see anything other than the hologram they project around themselves. The sun of their own existence blots out the stars, makes nonexistent the vastness of the spiritual Cosmos. At this time and in this way, they have self-selected themselves out of being chosen. Awakeness chooses the awake, the attentive, the searching.

The ones who are chosen do not have it easy. In some sense, it is easier to rest in the muffled world of societal complacency. Those chosen stand up out of that world; they walk the eternal path of wide and deep consciousness. Alone, yet aware of the great interflow of which they are a manifestation, the shoreless Ocean of which they are a wave. Alone, empty of all the world has to offer, dwelling in internal solitude, sometimes bereft of even the awareness of God's presence. Alone.

Yet standing.

RADIANCE

24
His disciples said to him,
"Show us the place where you are,
for we need to seek it."
He said to them,
"Whoever has ears, listen.
There is light within a person of light,
and it lights up the whole world.
If it does not shine, there is darkness."

"Come on, Jesus. We see your consciousness state. Tell us the place where you are to have such a point of view. We want to be in that place."

"Well then, listen up! I have light within me. I am not standing *in* the light. I AM the light, for it is inside me and it is who I am. As light, I light up all around me. If I am not light, there is only darkness."

The disciples have never met a person like Jesus. Everyone else was running around grumbling and mumbling about the state of the world, how dissension and turmoil were everywhere. (And with all their mumbling and grumbling, they were helping to produce the state of the world they abhorred).

Jesus is firmly in the world, facing and dealing with all he meets, yet he is not dark about it. At the core of his being is an open door to the light of Creation, the light radiating outward since the Beginning-of-It-All. Jesus knows he is that light, an embodying of that light. So are we when we identify with it (when we make ourselves identical to it).

This is not the light of light-versus-dark. This is the light that births both light and dark. When we are that light, all such dualities are resolved. We are in the world, but not of the world. We are coming from a different place, the place where Jesus is.

YOUR SOUL PUPIL

25

Jesus said,
"Love your brother as your own soul.
Guard him like the pupil of your eye."

Who is your brother? All those—regardless of gender or species or any other distinction—who come from the same womb. In other words: everything, for we were all formed in the Creator's womb. Jesus calls us to love all of creation as we love our own souls, including and especially the two-leggeds, who may be the hardest of all to love.

Your own soul: the very sweetness of your being, the deliciousness of You-the-Incomparable. That which emerges from the Wellspring, the living waters of Life. You, sweetheart, you!

This is different from loving our neighbors as our selves. Forget self, that part of you that kisses itself in its many mirrors, leaving lip prints on its own reflections. Love your neighbor as *your own soul*. This kicks it up a few notches; it throws Jesus' command into other dimensions.

Guard him like the pupil of your eye. The pupils of our eyes are the openings—the openness—that receive and emit light. As always, Jesus is speaking of the physical to explain the spiritual. Protect all of creation, including the two-leggeds, as you protect your spiritual eye: that openness of your soul that receives (and emits) the light of living love. Without it, we would live in spiritual darkness, an awful place of "weeping and wailing and gnashing of teeth."

The spiritual eye is a precious gift and must be protected. How is it protected? Through our continuous opening to the sight it gives: in-sight. "Protect all of creation as you protect your spiritual insight." If we are not protecting our spiritual insight, we are not doing very well by the rest of creation. As we go, so goes the universe.

What is this love we are asked to embody? Love is the Life Force animating the universe, calling us all into being, giving us life. We are this love embodying itself. When we shut it off, we are an ingrown hair, a carbuncle on the butt cheeks, an ulceration. This is the self at its most insidious and hideous.

When we personify love, embody love, we are open, free, filled with light. This light is the warmth and the heartiness of our Source.

LOG-ARHYTHM

26

Jesus said,
"You see the splinter in your brother's eye,
but you do not see the log in your own eye.
When you cast the log out of your own eye,
then you will see clearly
to cast the splinter from your brother's eye."

The splinter in my own eye of consciousness is like a beam of wood to me, affecting my entire vision. But I think it is just a splinter: no big deal. Or I may not even know I have a splinter at all. I have been living with this consciousness handicap for so long that I think it is normal.

I can certainly see where others have gone wrong, though. I can see what hinders their vision. If I'm not careful, I will sashay around, concerned about everyone else's splinters, while doing nothing about my chunk of wood.

When I remove this log of judgment from my eye, not only can I see a clear way for the removal of a splinter from another's eye, but the other will trust me to do so . . . and may perhaps do the same for me.

SLEEPING WITH A NIGHT LIGHT

27a
*"If you do not fast from the world,
you will not find the Kingdom."*

To fast means to abstain from, to not take in nourishment.

When our attention is focused on one thing, it does not and cannot notice other aspects of our surroundings. When our attention is focused on the world, on the human-created society, we do not and cannot see the Kingdom, the larger arena in which we live and move and have our being (and which simultaneously lives and moves within us and as us). We need to fast from all that distracts us from the Kingdom.

Some folk live within the all-night blazing light of a city and rarely see the stars or moon; they rarely hear the full richness of silence; they regard fasting from such noisome blaze as unthinkable, undesirable. A woman who hosts an inn in the nether realms of Arizona, a lovely place on a small lake way out nowhere, tells of a man who brought his family there. As night came, he asked if she would turn on the lights outside so they could walk around. She said there were no lights except for the stars and moon. He was indignant and fearful, packed their bags, and left in the safety of the morning, returning to the eternal hum and light of his city.

We do the same with our awareness, keeping the lights on and the sound going continuously. We blind ourselves to a larger reality we will never see unless we venture outside our little comfortable tents of manufactured light . . . into the darkness of the Kingdom.

KEEPING
THE SABBATH

27b
"If you do not keep the Sabbath as a Sabbath, you will not see the Father."

The Sabbath is traditionally on a Saturday. Some Christians, not all, got it confused with Sunday. From my point of view, the Sabbath is every day.

Keeping the Sabbath means to keep your soul in a place of rest, of repose, of freeness—no matter what is going on "outside." Some call this contemplation (con-templ-ation: living in the *templum*, the temple, the clear open space). Some call it mindfulness (open, calm awareness).

No matter what we call it, the Sabbath allows the calm "inside" to be our calm "outside," so that the inside and the outside are a single calm, open, vibrant experience, facing and dealing with all that is—because all that is, is all we is.

That's called seeing the Father, the Source, the Wellspring, the Mother, the Grandfather, the Grandmother, the Great Ah-Hoo-Ah-Hoo-Ah.

Seeing it is being it.

I FOUND ALL OF THEM DRUNK

28
Jesus said,
"I stood in the midst of the world,
and I came to them in the flesh.
I found all of them drunk;
I found none of them thirsty.
My soul was afflicted for humanity's children,
because they are blind in their hearts.
They do not see
that they came into the world empty,
and they will go out of the world empty.
But now they are drunk.
When they sober up, they will repent."

I stood in the midst of the world, and I came to them in the flesh. Past tense here, as if Jesus is reflecting back. He says, "I stood right in the middle of it all. I was meat, flesh like everyone else."

Who is this "I" that stands in the midst of us, that comes to us in the flesh? Anyone who bumps into Jesus has to resolve that question. Jesus has no question about it. He knows he is the Source embodying itself. He is neither mentally blind nor drunk like the rest of us. Jesus has a different consciousness state.

He takes his place in plain sight. Visible. But almost no one sees him. (And the few who do doubt their eyes from time to time.) Neither does Jesus hover above nor stand on the periphery of things, a silent observer. He stands smack-dab in the middle of it all. He makes his presence felt and known, so much so that he even shakes up "the authorities."

He also reveals that he had a sense of mission, of purpose: "I came to them." He is like an arrow shot at a target—and the arrow hits the bull's eye: *I stood in the midst of the world.*

What does he find here in the world? *I found all of them drunk.* Ordinary consciousness is drunk consciousness. We are drunk on our desires and our wants, our grievances and our discontents. Our consciousness is clouded with our own reflections. We see our selves—the little gods we have constructed in our own images—everywhere. We strut and fret and worry about our selves, our nonexistent selves that we have created since birth with smoke and mirrors. We are drunk.

I found none of them thirsty. Not a single one is thirsty for the consciousness—the awareness—that Jesus embodies. No one feels the need to shift out of ordinary consciousness. Not thirsty means to be completely satisfied with the consciousness state we have . . . and even more deeply drunk than that: not even aware there are other consciousness states more expansive.

My soul was afflicted for humanity's children, because they are blind in their hearts. We all know how "they" are mentally blind. We don't know how *we* are mentally blind. Nor do we even think we are. So what does Jesus mean? You think I'm going to answer that for you? Whatever I said, you would shrug off in one way or another. It's a Jesus koan. You have to answer it for yourself. Deep inside.

They do not see that they have come into the world empty and they will go out of the world empty. Well, I'll be darned. Here is the answer. Or is it? It's not an answer unless we know what it means. Is this the same as *sunyata* (the Buddhist concept of emptiness)? Is Jesus a closet Buddhist? Is this emptiness the result of *advaita*, the opening to the non-dual?

I think it's much simpler than that. We are mentally, spiritually blind because we stand in our own light, casting our own shadows. We are full of ourselves. We came into the world empty, and then with the help of others, we created little selves we preen and cherish, protect and lay on the couches of learned doctors to get to the bottom of. We spend the time between when we came into the world (empty) and go out of the world (empty) licking our own fur, totally self-absorbed.

When they sober up, they will repent. We are drunk on desire, drunk on "the news," drunk on politics, drunk on entertainment, drunk on meditation and prayer, drunk on self-image, drunk on anger, drunk on being holy, drunk on education, drunk on money, drunk on security, drunk on insecurity, drunk on the now, drunk on the sweet bye-and-bye, drunk on her, drunk on him, drunk on if-I-could-just-get-that, drunk on if-I-could-just-get-rid-of-this, drunk on sex, drunk on abstaining from sex, drunk on rebelling, drunk on food, drunk on anything we can get drunk on.

The picture I get is of Jesus standing there in the midst of all this drunkenness, seeing it for what it is . . . and then with great fortitude, insight, compassion, and trust, saying, "Ah well, when they stop being mentally blind, they won't go back to that anymore."

THE CHICKEN OR THE EGG

29
Jesus said,
"If the flesh came into being because of spirit,
it is a wonder.
But if spirit came into being because of the body,
it is a wonder of wonders.
Indeed, I am amazed at how this great wealth
has made its home in this poverty."

Which came first, the mind or the body? Which produces the other? We continue to make that a controversy today. The biomechanics say there is no mind without the body. When the body goes, the mind goes. The more sane biomechanics say they don't know; this "no body = no mind" position is at best a point of view within the bounds and limitations of the biomechanical thought system.

Jesus directly addressed this issue. He regards each of these two understandings (and a third one, which he initiates) as marvelous, as causing one to gasp in wonder. If the body came into being because of mind, that is astonishing (a wonder). If the mind came into being because of body, that is even more astonishing (a wonder of wonders). So far, Jesus has not taken a position (unless we substitute "incredulous" for the word "amazed").

With the word "but" comes a third viewpoint or understanding. Jesus says we can marvel over the first two perspectives, but what he marvels at is outside these two divisive statements that war against each other. He is more interested in how it happens: *how this great wealth has made its home in this poverty.*

What is "this great wealth"? It is certainly not the rational syllogistic mind based upon duality, wonderful as it is. The great wealth Jesus is talking about is the Life Force itself, that great stream of Being that produces all. It expresses Itself in this poverty, this "clay," this earth matter that walks around, that flies, that creeps, that crawls.

What is more astonishing than the chicken-egg, mind-body question is that we—and all that exist—are embodiments of the Life Force Itself. When we truly grasp that, we are transformed. Our consciousness shifts into a more marvelous realm.

GOD ENERGY

30
Jesus said,
"Where there are three gods, they are gods.
Where there are two or one,
I am with that one."

Numbers are important. They show relationship. "Two is company," we say, "but three is a crowd." Jesus, quoting a psalm (82), said, "You are gods." When we are two gods conversing or one god standing alone, all the energy that Jesus represents is with us. When we triplicate, that energy shoots off into the heavens, somewhere complex and theological.

HOMETOWN STUPOR

31
Jesus said,
"No prophet is accepted in his own village;
no physician heals those who know him."

In our twenty-first century, we have a fair idea of what a physician is, but our image of a prophet is a cartoon character on a street corner with a sign saying that the world is ending.

What is a prophet? Here is what that old prophet, Abraham Heschel, had to say: Prophets are "some of the most disturbing people who ever lived." A prophet is "endowed with a mission, with the power of a word not his own . . . The prophet's task is to convey a divine view, yet as a person he IS a point of view. He speaks from the perspective of God as perceived from the perspective of his own situation. . . The prophet is not only a prophet. He is also poet, preacher, patriot, statesman, social critic, moralist" (*The Prophets*, pp. xxi–xxii).

A prophet's consciousness has expanded far beyond ordinary consciousness. Ordinary consciousness is centered in the body and its desires, in human-created social reality. A prophet's consciousness is centered in the wider realms of the Cosmos. A prophet is a seer and a hearer of the unfolding energies of our Source. A prophet is compelled to speak, cannot *not* speak what he sees and hears, what he *knows*.

Jesus said, from his own experience, that a prophet is not accepted as a prophet by those who grew up with him, the people in his hometown. "Oh," we think, "that's just Jesus rattling on again!"

We are odd ducks. We grow to distrust the familiar. We have a hardening of our categories. We go running after someone or something over there somewhere. The exotic—the new!—must have what we are looking for.

(Someone told me some years back that there was a guru a couple of states away and I should go see him. I said if he is a guru, he knows where I live. I had learned by that time to listen to the inner voice, that which was most familiar.)

To hear truth, to be healed (made whole, made holy, made healthy), we only need to open ourselves to what is immediately around us and within our own hearts. The sphere of immediacy in which we live is our only opportunity for healing. We don't have to go anywhere.

THE HIGH MOUNTAIN

32
Jesus said,
"A city built and fortified on a high mountain cannot be taken, nor can it be hidden."

In-spire means "breathe in." Expire means "breathe out." To aspire means "look to become the highest breath possible." Spiritual (spire-itual) aspiration is a doubly reinforced concentration on opening to the Highest Breath and Its Breathing.

As we become more stable (e-stabl-ished) there, when we build and fortify our city there, we cannot be taken down by anyone or any force. Nor can the Light that shines from that Breathing be hidden.

Our treasures (all that we value) are "laid up in Heaven."

HOUSETOP PREACHING

33a
Jesus said,
"What you hear in your ears
preach from your housetop."

We have physical ears and spiritual ears. We hear the sounds of traffic in both realms. Spiritual ear traffic blares at us in the form of cognitive-emotional thought, intuition, and imagery. Those three can arrive melded into a single packet.

Thought "packets" that pass through our consciousness—our awareness—consist of one part cognition and one part emotion. Every thought is loaded with emotional juice. There is no such thing as dry thought. Every thought we have produces an instant physiological effect in the body. The thought body and the physical body interflow.

Thoughts are sometimes accompanied with flashes of intuition and vivid imagery. We may hear and see what someone sitting next to us does not hear or see at all. This is discernibly different from everyday chit-chat (the rooftop chatter, as some Buddhists call it).

What we hear in our spiritual ears we are to speak aloud. We are to say what we hear. How do we do this? Seventy-five to 85 percent of our communication with others is nonverbal. The *way* we say something communicates more than the typed-out text of what we say. It is the delivery that counts the most. Facial expression, eye contact, gestures, body posture, voice tone and rhythm, and other more subtle nonverbal cues clue others into our meaning.

The most subtle realm of all is the spiritual realm, the realm of the Life Force, that which we embody, which calls us into being at every moment, every nanosecond. This is the realm of the spiritual ear. This is the core of our being. We preach it from the housetop all the time. We preach it through the nonverbal channels. Each of us is perfectly transparent. Who we are (what we hear in our ears) radiates outward in all directions all the time.

BASKET CASES

33b
"For no one lights a lamp
and puts it under a bushel basket
or in a hidden place.
Rather, the lamp is placed on a stand
so that everyone who goes in and out
will see its light."

We believe we are bushel baskets. Light beings, we weave ourselves clothing—and then insist that we dare not be naked light, shining unadorned. In trying to make our selves somebodies, as Jesus says, we become nobodies.

Our consciousness is light, the light of awareness. Awareness courses through the heart-brain and the head-brain. The light of awareness is seen as the nimbus (whole-being aura) and the halo (head aura). The bushel basket of petulance—of self-absorption, of singing the song of me, me, me—is left behind, vanquished, tootle-ooed.

We shine.

DITCHING OUR LIVES

34
Jesus said,
"If a blind person leads another blind person,
they will both fall into a pit."

Thought and imagery are fine. They arise naturally. They also disappear naturally. When we do not let them disappear, we are blind, stuck in obscuration. We cannot see the vast openness that we are and in which we dwell. We lead ourselves into a pit—a comfortable pit, an old familiar pit, but a pit nonetheless.

Trapped in images of the past, old thoughts suck your energy. Caught in movies of the immediate and distant future, you ditch yourself and are not here. Sitting entranced in the present moment(um), you are snug within your ditch. The part of you that leads and the part of you that follows are both sunk, caught in a time-space warp of your own making.

PHAT! Break free! Wake up! Be aware.

TYING OUR HANDS
OF AWARENESS

35
Jesus said,
"No one can enter the house of a strong man
and take it by force
unless he ties the strong man's hands.
Then the thief can loot his house."

The hands of discernment—of thought, of intuition—must be open and empty, clean and receptive for spiritual understanding to occur. Above all, these hands of attention and receptivity must be readily available; they can't be clenched fists stuffed in our pockets.

If our house of consciousness is to be robbed, its treasures and wealth stolen from us, our hands of awareness must first be bound. Our consciousness then exists only on a superficial level, attentive to the surface of life, unable to dive into its depths of meaning.

Who are the thieves who tie our hands but ourselves? We stand bound within our own houses, victims of any passing fancy, doubt, or worry that comes along. A mind given to distraction is a thief, robbing us of contemplative awareness; this thief steals from us our residence in the templum—the clear open space of understanding. We are robbed of knowing our place in the Cosmos; our ever-deepening appreciation of our Source, our love for Life's blooming, has been plundered. We tie our own hands and sit captive in our households.

CLOTHES
GET IN THE WAY

36
Jesus said,
"Do not worry from morning until evening
and from evening until morning
with what you're going to wear."

We choose our conceptual, spiritual, philosophical, and metaphysical garbs. We clothe our naked souls. If we're not careful, we then begin to think that our packaging is the gift, that the container is the content. (In Zen terms, we row our boat to the other shore, pick up the boat, and carry it. Now the boat is rowing us.)

Do not worry all day long and all night long whether you are wearing the correct doctrinal garb. Every story we tell ourselves is just that—a story—and at its best, a passageway into our continuous rebirthing.

Trample your clothes under your feet, says Jesus in his next saying. No need to build social clubs around your particular chosen form of clothing; don't bother creating clusters of folks all wearing the same uniform.

We each stand naked before our Source. When we know that we are the Source sourcing, clothes just get in the way.

THE SON OF THE LIVING ONE

37
His disciples asked him,
"When will you become revealed to us?
When will we see you?"
Jesus replied,
"When you strip naked without being ashamed
and trample your clothes under your feet
like little children do,
then will you see the Son of the Living One,
without being afraid."

What strange questions these warriors-of-spirit-in-training (disciples) are asking. Isn't Jesus standing right in front of them? Aren't they looking right at him?

When will you become revealed to us? Here, the burden of effort lies upon Jesus. When is *he* going to do something? When is he going to reveal himself as "the son of the Living One" to their physical senses?

We are like that. We impatiently ask for the heavens to roll back and for True Reality to be revealed. If this does not happen (on our schedule), we can get pretty snarky.

"When" questions are always about time; people living in the realm of time ask these sorts of questions. The disciples are wanting the timeless to appear in the realm of time. And right now, please!

With the disciples' second question, they put the focus on themselves: *When will we see you?* Again, we hear their impatience. However, the question could be rephrased (and perhaps some of them mean it this way): "What do we have to do to see you as you are in the spiritual realm, in the realm of the timeless?"

This is a more practical training question. Jesus gives them a direct answer, direct, that is, if we are standing in a place of consciousness where we can hear it. First, we have to take off all our clothing without shame and trample it underfoot just as a child does.

We clothe ourselves in ideas, beliefs, doctrine, theory, expectations, requirements, feelings, demands, holiness, righteousness, despair, degradation, whining, greed, desire, pleasure, pain, anger, sorrow, and ten thousand other shades of wear. But Jesus said if we want to see the Son of the Living One without fear, we too must become an offspring of the Living One. We must stand naked in the universe, attached to nothing, clinging to nothing, becoming as nothing.

We cannot even cling to nothingness, for a religion can be made of nothingness, and then—*pow!*—we are clothed once again.

ISOMETRICS
OF THE SOUL

38
Jesus said,
"Many times you've longed
to hear these words I am saying to you,
and you have no one else
from whom you can hear them.
There will be days when you look for me
and you won't be able to find me."

We look for a guide. No instruction booklet was attached to our umbilical cord. Where are we? Who are we? What's going on? Sometimes we don't think about it, but often we want some answers. We want some understanding.

Many times you've longed to hear these words I am saying to you. Jesus has been ruthlessly passing out understanding. He speaks directly and also with parables. His words are like a sharp sword, like a depth charge. These are the words folk have been waiting to hear, wanting to hear.

You have no one else from whom you can hear them. Jesus is the only one who speaks the way he does. No one else is walking around speaking the truth he is proclaiming: We are children of the Living God, offspring of the Wellspring. We are known and seen and loved.

There will be days when you will look for me and you won't be able to find me. This is sometimes known as the dark night of the soul. At times we feel lost and abandoned. We cannot find grace and mercy anywhere. We do not feel Christ-consciousness. Jesus is nowhere to be found. This is the nature of human life. It is an isometrics of the soul, producing greater strength through the flexing and releasing of opposing muscles. Lost-found, discouraged-encouraged, despairing-joyous. This is the way we become more and more spiritually "toned," until such extremes are no longer necessary. As long as we are embodying, however, this spiritual training continues.

We listen to the words of Jesus. He speaks truth.

PROFESSIONAL RELIGIONISTS

39a
Jesus said,
"The Pharisees and the scribes
have taken the keys of knowledge
and hidden them.
They themselves do not enter,
nor do they allow those who wish to."

Those who rely on literal or surface interpretation of sacred writings and those who are professional religionists hide the keys to knowledge or deeper understanding from themselves and from others. They do not "enter"—they do not allow the writings and the wisdom they veil to merge with their souls—but instead, they stand outside and merely look through the windows, untouched. Insisting that their scholastic and doctrinal endeavors are The Truth, they keep those who yield to their authority from deep experiential knowing. Jesus sees their game.

Of course, the same thing happens with Jesus' sayings.

THE SNAKE-DOVE COMBO

39b
*"Be wise as snakes
and as innocent as doves."*

When our psychic skins are too tight, when our souls are suffocating, when those suits of socio-spiritual clothes we put on each day are so unbecomingly small, it's time to shed our snake skins and let what cannot be contained burst into new life.

We need not be afraid. We will contain it soon enough.

When we experience the unlimited expansion of soul and spirit, we will find ourselves as gentle and as innocent as doves.

ROOTING OURSELVES IN THE TRICKY TRIO

40

Jesus said,
"A grapevine has been planted outside of the Father,
but since it is unsupported,
it will be pulled up by its roots and it will die."

Consider that we are the grapevine. Our attention is our root tip seeking nourishment, soul food. We can place our attention where we wish. If our habit is to place our attention "outside of the Father," we will not grow strong. We can be easily pulled up by our roots.

The Father is the Source of all being, the Wellspring, the Formless-Always-Forming, that which does not perish.

What does perish? Mister Buddha called it right: greed, hostility, and stupor—the tricky trio. They are outside the Father. We create them ourselves. They are based on fear and its resultant clinging. We sink our roots in them. Greed is an insatiable hunger for security. Hostility is the protection of our own turf, our own greed pile. Stupor is zoning out.

We look to build our own little cosmos within the Cosmos. Like the man who built his house on sand, though, it will all be washed away. Using the grapevine metaphor, it will be uprooted. One slight tug, and up it comes.

If we want Everlasting, we must plant in the Everlasting. We must turn our attention to the One-Who-Breathes-Us.

THE MORE, THE MORE AND THE LESS, THE LESS

41

Jesus said,
"Whoever has something in hand will receive more,
and whoever has nothing
will be deprived of even that little bit."

Jesus is not a man of possessions. He owns nothing but the clothes he wears, and he is not attached even to those; he is willing to give them away. So why does he speak here of an increase of possessions?

His words could be taken as prophetic of today's world where the rich get richer and the poor get poorer. Prophecy is not an expression of approval, however; Jesus is not saying he's in favor of wealthy folk having advantages, while the destitute lose what little they have. We know Jesus' stance on money: he said that the widow who gave two mites (the smallest coins of the time) gave more than the richest philanthropists, partly because she gave all she had.

In any case, Jesus is speaking of something other than this world's riches. This is not a prophecy but a spiritual truth: *Whoever has something in hand will receive more.* When we open ourselves to the mercy, love, judgment, compassion, and mystery of the realm of spirit (Jesus often called it the Kingdom of Heaven), we will be given more access to its energies and its understandings. The more we open to it, the more it opens to us. The more we possess, the more we are given.

Jesus said the contrary is also true: *Whoever has nothing will be deprived of even that little bit.* When we take small sips of air rather than breathing deeply, over time we become almost incapable of taking a deep breath. We do this to ourselves. The same is true in the realm of spirit. When we choose not to breathe that stronger, purer air, what little of it we possess, along with our ability to breathe it, will be taken away.

We are mind, body, and spirit. In today's world, we think it profitable to exercise the mind and the body. We trot them around. We flex and stretch them. It is necessary to do the same with spirit. If we neglect to exercise our relationship with our Source, with That which gives us being, from Whom we came and to Whom we shall return, what little relationship we have will fall away.

The good news is that the more we open ourselves to a close relationship with the Life Force—with God, our Progenitor, our Source—the more capacity we have for this relationship, and the greater it grows. Friendship begets friendship.

And that, my dears, is a happy, happy thing.

ONE
OF THOSE

42
Jesus said,
"Be one of those who pass by."

Do not become entangled. Block no orifices with residue. Move on. Go straight ahead. No tumbling around in the dryer of your mind. No lint collection. Step in and meet and greet whatever comes—and send it on its way. Stop trying to fix the world. Simply be you. Keep moving. No velcro mind. All images are chimera. Keep breathing. Inhale, and then exhale.

Be one of those who pass on by.

SHOW US
YOUR CREDENTIALS

43
His disciples asked him,
"Who are you,
that you should say these things to us?"
Jesus answered,
"Don't you recognize who I am
from what I say to you?
You have become like the Jews
who either love the tree and hate its fruit,
or love the fruit and hate the tree."

No one talks the way Jesus talks. He is a mythopoet of the highest order. He speaks with absolute assurance of the Absolute. Unlike others who seem to slip in and out of Now, Jesus is totally present. He seems to rely entirely on the Tao Flow, which he sometimes addresses as Father. He is a good teacher, speaking in parables and metaphors that set off explosions of inner awareness.

His students, though, sometimes get a little riled. They want a course outline; they want to know if he's grading on the curve. They want to know who the heck he is to say such things and who's the person behind the words (not realizing that Jesus and the words he speaks are one and the same).

Jesus calls them on it. *Don't you recognize who I am from what I say to you?* He tells them they are like people who like a tree but loathe its fruit, or they like the fruit but loathe the tree. Some of the folk that follow Jesus around like his powerful personality, but they don't particularly care for what he's saying. Others know his words quench their spiritual thirst, but they wonder about his rustic bastardly background. "Can any good thing come out of Nazareth?" they ask.

Of course, some of the folks close to Jesus like both who he is and what he says. Whether looking at Jesus or listening to him, they never see or hear anything but a seamless Whole. These folk don't talk much in class, but every once in a while Jesus pulls them aside and tells them a few more things.

SPIRITUAL SUICIDE

44
Jesus said,
"Whoever blasphemes against the Father
will be forgiven,
and whoever blasphemes against the Son
will be forgiven,
but whoever blasphemes against the Holy Spirit
will not be forgiven either on earth or in heaven."

Blaspheme means to curse, to revile, to execrate, to make not sacred. Profane means to stand outside the temple (profanum). Blaspheme takes it a step further by standing outside the temple and actively sending curses to it from one's heart.

Jesus says we can curse our Source and all the manifestations and embodyings of our Source—and that angry hatred and railing sent outward from the depths of our hearts will be forgiven. We can recover from that heart attack. We can be released from that stance and come back into favor with ourselves and our Source.

Not so if we blaspheme the Holy Spirit. We cannot send bitter invective inward against the Life Force that creates us—that calls us into being each moment, each nanosecond—and live. We become bitter shrunken creatures cut off from the Spirit of Life itself. We are like wells that poisons themselves. We sit in our own poison and are of no use or good for anyone, including ourselves. We are unforgiven.

Notice that we do this to ourselves. We are cursed from within our own being by damning (damming) the Life Force that flows through us. It is like a bud of a fractal cursing the flow of the Great Fractal that brought it into being. It shrivels and dies. Not even the Great Fractal can forgive (release) it. It is a grape that has died on the vine by the powers of its own will.

This saying tells us that we can opt out of the Game. Our hearts, through our own repeated efforts, can become so hardened that we are never heard from again. That's what it means to be unforgiven.

GRAPES, THORNS, FIGS, AND THISTLES

45

Jesus said,
"Grapes are not harvested from thorns,
nor are figs gathered from thistles,
for they do not produce fruit.
Good people bring good things
out of their storehouses;
bad people bring evil things out of their storehouses,
and they say evil things.
For from the overflow of their hearts
come evil things."

Every move we make proclaims the quality of who we are. Every thought, every nuance of the psyche, of the soul, reverberates and transforms our essence, the quality of our sphere of energy, and thereby the entire Cosmos.

When thorns and thistles grow in our heart-minds, they produce a crown of thorns, which we press upon our heads and on the heads of those around us. We suffer and are insufferable.

The production of succulent fruit requires our opening ourselves as conduits, conductors of the creative juice of life. When the conduit and the juice become one, new universes of creativity and daring are born. How can new fruit be born—except by throwing the entire tree, the entire Cosmos into the endeavor?

JUICED

46
Jesus said,
"Among those born of woman,
from Adam until John the Baptist,
there is no one who is above John the Baptist,
so that he should not lower his eyes before him.
But I have said whoever of you becomes like a child
will know the Kingdom
and will be greater than John."

Somewhere along the way we start to suspect that the world does not have all the answers; it may not even have the right questions.

During childhood, we knew intimately our realms of imagination, the creative imagery that manifested at times in surprising ways, bursting into the world as poetry of invention. If we begin to trust this realm more, we live in the realm of Spirit, of in-spire-ation: the breathing in of creation's energies and the breathing out of its material and spiritual effects.

We rejoice. We are tapped into the Juice. We re-juice. This is the Kingdom. We are infants at play in the energetic realm of our Source, the Great Mystery, our Father and our Mother. Born of woman, we are now born of Spirit. We are greater than John—but greater than and less than no longer matter.

HORSE-RIDING JESUS

47a
Jesus said,
"A person cannot ride two horses at once,
nor stretch two bows."

Who is this horse-riding Jesus? Isn't he supposed to dangle his legs from a donkey, all meek and lowly? No matter. He is who he is.

He says on another occasion, "Let the light of your eye be single." Whatever you are doing, do it with your whole heart and mind and soul. No vacillation. No shifting from one foot to another. Firm stride forward.

It starts from inside, you know, this whole business of trying to ride two horses at once, the attempted stretching of two bows. And I speak not here of multitasking. I speak of all that which moves us away from singleness of spirit. We cannot serve two masters. We cannot serve the contraction of ourselves while serving the vastness that we are.

ONE MASTER

47b
"Nor is it possible for a servant to serve two masters.
If he tries, he will honor the one
and treat the other contemptuously."

Many spiritual paths exist, all leading to the same Opening. Each path has a master of that path, a person who has proven the validity of the path through his or her very being, through action, word, and presence. We can be aware of all paths and learn from them, but to follow more than one master of a path diffuses the one-pointedness that is essential for merging with the master. We set our whole hearts on one master, become attuned to and identical with that master's wisdom and compassion.

THE VINTAGE
AND THE FRESH

47c
*"No one drinks vintage wine
and immediately wants to drink fresh wine."*

Fresh wine is the raw experience of physically based consciousness. Vintage wine is the rarefied and entrancing atmosphere of the invisible. We tend to call the first—the realm of brute consciousness—"real," while we call the realm of vintage wine—the realm of spirit—"imaginary."

What we call imaginary, however, is actually the fruition of what we call real: the vintage is a refinement of the fresh. Paradoxically, the vintage also births the fresh. Since they birth each other, the distinctions we make between the two are arbitrary; they show our inability and unwillingness to allow the dissolution of their boundaries.

When we cast our lot with the realm of the invisible—of spirit—we may not wish to return to the realm of the visible. We wish to keep sipping that heavenly wine. But here and now, at this time, we are embodying. We are fresh wine. We ask to let this cup pass from us, but we must drink it.

VINTAGE WINE
AND THE ROBE WITH NO SEAMS

47d
"New wine is not put into old wineskins,
lest they burst.
Vintage wine is not put into new wineskins,
lest it be spoiled.
An old patch is not sewn onto a new garment,
because it would tear."

A vintage wine is one whose parts—its chemical constituents—are moving in harmony. Accustomed to their interplay with one another, they delight in each other. At one time, both were fresh and thus well matched, and now they have aged together.

The wine of spirit is the wine of understanding and awareness. Deep understanding cannot be put into a new container, into a consciousness not capable of containing it. Nor can a supra-ordinate consciousness abide with shallow linear and literal understandings. The deep truths of spirit are received only by those who deepen with them.

Cloth from the robe with no seams cannot be used to stitch up a seamed garment. The one must be abandoned for the other.

MOVING MOUNTAINS

48

*Jesus said,
"If two can make peace with each other
in a single house,
they will say to the mountain, 'Move!'
and it will move."*

When we have a split mind, we can do nothing. When we are caught in our dualistic (duelistic) nature—me-you, us-them, good-bad—we are much less powerful than when "the light of our eye is single."

Single does not mean we choose one pole of our dualistic ladder and use it as our spiritual pogo stick. Instead, we transcend the ladder—and then, as in Jacob's dream, we identify with the angels that ascend and descend freely upon it.

And then we will see that all mountains are already moving.

THE EYE OF THE ETERNAL

49
Jesus said,
"Blessed are the single ones and the chosen,
for you will find the Kingdom.
You emerged from it,
and to it you will return."

The Kingdom is the eternal. The world is the temporal. When we are born into this world, we are born into a constriction of time and space. We condensate, become dense. We lose our way, we fall for it.

But we will find the Kingdom. We will find the eternal, our true home. We emerged from it and we will return to it. Now. While we are consciously aware.

We are in the world but not of the world, and we will know it. How? By becoming a singular eye, releasing the distraction of the two eyes of the world, which look first here, now there. To see the eternal, we must have the eye of the eternal.

Whatever we attend to, we become. We are chosen as we choose. With the eye of the eternal and the choosing of the eternal, we find the Kingdom. We emerged from it—and now we return.

WHERE ARE YOU FROM?

50a
Jesus said,
"If they ask,
'Where did you come from?'
say to them,
'We came from the light,
the place where the light is produced from itself.
It established itself
and revealed itself in their image.'"

When I was pedaling my bicycle across parts of the United States some years ago, folk would ask, "Where are you from?" and I would answer, "I come from my mother's womb." Jesus has a better answer, zooming back into time where there was no time: *We came from the light, the place where the light is produced from itself.*

One reason Jesus is so far ahead of the consciousness of his time is that his awareness is outside time. He recommends that his students (those who studied his way of being) come from the same place: the place where light came into being all by itself. The Origin. The Source.

We can all reach back into our genealogy and track our ancestral flow through time. Some of us can even feel our ancestors looking through our eyes. Jesus said go further, zoom further back: go back, not just in intellect, but in experience, to the place where light is produced from itself. Feel that place looking through your eyes.

He adds an even more startling statement: *It established itself and revealed itself in their image.* Here he does not speak of "the Father." He speaks of the light establishing itself and continues speaking of "it." No gender here. This is before gender. It established itself and became manifest.

This is Meister Eckhart's Godhead. This is Hinduism's *Tat Tvam Asi* (Thou Art That). This is the Source, the Origin, the Wellspring out of which all flows, even the conception of Itself as God the Father. This is Ibn Arabi's "self-disclosure of God."

And there is more: *It revealed itself in their image.* Further mystery. Jesus does not say: It came and revealed itself in *its* image, but in *their* image. In whose image? Who is this "their"?

The Genesis story speaks of the creation of humans in this way: "Let us make people in our image." This "us" and "our" is the "their" Jesus refers to. This is a mystery. We come out of Mystery, a mystery that is not just a singular oneness as we trap ourselves into believing, but a community, a communion forming a oneness. We are made in the image of this Mystery.

Where are we from? We are from the place where light is produced from itself. We exist because it came and revealed itself in its own image. We are that revelation.

EMBODYING THE LIGHT

50b
"If they ask you,
'Are you it?'
say, 'We are its children.
We are the chosen ones of the Living Father.'"

"It" refers, as pointed out in the first part of this saying (50a), to the light that is produced from itself. Jesus says here that if we are asked, "Are you that light?" we should reply that we are the light's chosen offspring. We come from the light that is produced from itself.

This is our Origin. This is not something that happened way long ago, and we are an extenuated result. This light, our Father, our Source, is happening now, and we are its embodying.

We are the light of the world. We dis-remember and plunge ourselves into our melodramas. And yet, even these melodramas are the eternal light shining into and out of darkness. At this moment now, we are the chosen ones; we are embodyings of the living Light that is produced from Itself.

THE SIGN
WITHIN YOU

50c

"If they ask you,
'What is the sign within you of your Father?'
say to them,
'It is movement. It is rest.'"

We move as the Spirit moves. We rest as the Spirit rests. We are of our Father, whose Spirit is a wind that both flows and is still. We follow that Spirit, that Tao flow. It is the sign within us of our Father, of our Source.

This sign within us is a binary code, movement (1) and rest (0). Through the 1 of movement and the 0 of repose, all systems are built. All other numbers come into play, to infinity and beyond. All creation emerges through this movement and this rest.

Movement and rest are the Breath of the Father. The two movements—inhalation and exhalation—are conjoined by a pause, a rest. All reality, all truth is created through and subsists upon this movement and this rest.

WHAT ARE WE WAITING FOR?

51
His disciples asked him,
"When will the dead rest?
When will the new world arrive?"
He replied,
"It has already come,
but you do not recognize it."

The disciples often confuse themselves by making a distinction between the external world and the internal world. They have not opened themselves to the consciousness of Jesus.

They have two major concerns here, which are really one concern. They are looking for a new world, a world long promised, in which their ancestors could finally find peace instead of dwelling in a place of the in-between. The coming of a dead-resting new world was a prevalent view at that time in their culture.

We are no different today. Each of us is born into a particular worldview, and each of us adopts that view as our own. Then we work within the frame of that worldview to resolve its designated problems.

Most worldviews are dualistic in nature. We experience the world as this-and-that, self-and-other, now-and-then. This is called common sense and is generally not disputed. Its effect, however, is similar to that of Humpty Dumpty who had a great fall and could not be put back together again by the king's greatest technology and manpower.

Jesus said, "That which you are waiting for has come, but you don't recognize it." When we take off the virtual-reality helmet we have been wearing since birth—the helmet of dualistic views, of split vision—we open to the splendid world of infinity in every direction and no separation. We stop looking to recognize (re-cognize) it: we go out of our little cognitive minds, and we see that we are already here and have always already been here.

We burst into laughter.

THE LIVING ONE
WHO IS WITH YOU

52
His disciples said to him,
"Twenty-four prophets spoke in Israel,
and all of them spoke of you."
He said to them,
"You have deserted the living one in your presence,
and you're speaking only of the dead."

The disciples have already formed a theology here: they are saying that the entire Hebrew Bible (the twenty-four prophets that spoke to the Hebrew people) is pointing directly to Jesus. (The Hebrew Bible, the Tanakh—what Christians call the Old Testament—consists of twenty-four books: the Torah, the Prophets [Joshua, Judges, 1 Samuel, 2 Samuel, 1 Kings, 2 Kings, Isaiah, Jeremiah, Ezekiel, The Twelve Prophets], and the Writings [Psalms, Proverbs, Job, The Song of Songs, Ruth, Lamentations, Ecclesiastes, Esther, Daniel, Ezra, Nehemiah, 1 Chronicles, 2 Chronicles].)

Jesus understood and respected the Tanakh. He was invited to read from it and comment upon it in the synagogues. Jesus was the one who convinced the disciples that the prophecies of the Tanakh pointed toward him:

> And he came to Nazareth, where he had been brought up. And as was his custom, he went to the synagogue on the Sabbath day, and he stood up to read. And the scroll of the prophet Isaiah was given to him. He unrolled the scroll and found the place where it was written,
>
> "The Spirit of the Lord is upon me,
> because he has anointed me
> to proclaim good news to the poor.
> He has sent me to proclaim liberty to the captives
> and recovering of sight to the blind,
> to set at liberty those who are oppressed,
> to proclaim the year of the Lord's favor."
>
> And he rolled up the scroll and gave it back to the attendant and sat down. And the eyes of all in the synagogue were fixed on him. And he began to say to them, "Today this Scripture has been fulfilled in your hearing." (Luke 4:16–21)

Jesus respected history; he used history to help his followers understand him and his teachings. But once that point was made, he focused on the immediacy of now. His disciples (those following his discipline) were looking back, like Lot's wife (who turned to a stationary pillar of salt because of her backward focus). Now Jesus is disciplining his friends (discipleing them): "You have deserted the living one who is with you."

We need to understand the past—but we are not to dwell there. Even a nanosecond ago is gone. We are to live here, NOW, with our inbreathing and out-breathing. This is the place of action, the creative and cutting edge of the unfolding universe. Here. Now.

We have heard this so often that it becomes a lifeless mantra. We acknowledge its truth and go on with our ruminations on the past. Rather than letting the dead bury the dead, we leave this living openness and join in the deadly burying.

We have omitted the Living One—even though he is present here with us—from our thoughts and conversation, while we have focused only on the dead.

CIRCUMCISION IN THE SPIRIT

53

His disciples said to him,
"Is circumcision beneficial or not?"
He answered them, "If it were beneficial,
you would be born already circumcised.
Rather, true circumcision in spirit
is entirely beneficial."

Jesus was never one to waste a metaphor. *Circum* means all the way around (circle). *Cision* means cut. An incision is a cutting into. An excision is a cutting out. Circumcision is cutting all the way around. Jesus says that physical circumcision is not useful. It is true circumcision in the spirit that is more than useful; it is "entirely beneficial."

We are to be in the world but not of the world. We are to be "passersby." This is cutting all the way around. As long as we have one piece of spiritual foreskin attached to the world of desire, the realm of *samsara*, as the Buddhists call it, we are in danger of infection. In fact, the attachment is the infection. We are to make the cut all the way around. No attachment.

Letting go of our attachments is painful but essential. If we wish to launch into the consciousness that Jesus knows and represents, we must cast off all lines that hold our spiritual vehicle to the world. This is completely beneficial. We are in the world, but not of the world.

BLESSED POORNESS

54
*Jesus said,
"Blessed are the poor,
for yours is the Kingdom of Heaven."*

In the material realm, poor means we do not have much in the way of worldly sustenance. In the realm of spirit, poor means we are not attached to anything. We act without attachment to the action or to the fruit of the action. We love without attachment. (If there is attachment, this is not love, but a selfish clinging.)

We are poor, stripped of all clothing of psychological and spiritual identity. We gain entry into the Kingdom of Heaven by gaining nothing and losing everything. Now we have gained everything and lost nothing.

The Kingdom of Heaven is a state of consciousness that is eternal.

"HE IS OUT OF HIS MIND"

55

Jesus said,
"Whoever does not hate father and mother
cannot be my disciple.
Whoever does not hate brothers and sisters
and bear the cross as I do
will not be worthy of me."

Jesus blazed a trail. He describes it to us here: "Turn away from—shun, do not adopt—the consciousness state—the mindset—of your mother and your father, nor of any others who were born before you. Don't conform to the mindset of your peers: your brothers and your sisters." This makes you a consciousness-orphan, a stranger in a strange land. This is a cross to bear. Everyone else fits in. You do not.

The fathers and mothers, brothers and sisters will even worship Jesus in a mindset you do not have. This is peculiar and paradoxical. To be worthy of Jesus, you do not adopt that mindset.

What kind of consciousness state or mindset do you have? What kind of consciousness state is worthy of the consciousness state of Jesus? One that is empty (kenotic) and open, without any of the preconceptions inculcated by the prepackaged Jesus of yore or the spin put on Jesus by the salvationists of today.

We embody the same consciousness that Jesus embodies. Be prepared! As you do this, the same thing is likely to happen to you that happened to Jesus: "And when his family heard it, they went to seize him, for they were saying, 'He is out of his mind'" (Mark 3:21).

We are no longer citizens of the world. We are an embodying of the Source, citizens of a world not seen by nor limited by the physical senses. We are in the world, but not of the world. We have left ordinary consciousness and opened to universal consciousness.

The consciousness state of Jesus is similar to that of Buddha and of Lao Tzu. Those fellows called this type of consciousness "embodying the light."

DOTE AND ANTIDOTE

56

*Jesus said,
"Whoever has come to know the world
has found only a corpse,
If someone has found that corpse
the world is not worthy of that person."*

Necrophilia means making love with a corpse. Unthinkable for most of us. Our minds rise up in revulsion and judgment. And yet we make love to the world. We do our best to revive its corpse with our ardor. "Wake up, world! Notice me!"

The world does not care. It is dead. We can make ourselves dead too when we dote on the world's "dote"—its poison. The "dote" of the world is made of three parts: greed, hatred, ignoreance. This mixture is deadly. Even, perhaps especially, in its homeopathic form: a teeny bit of greed, a speck of dislike, and a morsel of ignorance poisons the whole system.

The anti-dote is well known. All that is needed is its application: generosity, loving kindness, awareness.

When we become the antidote, we are no longer caressing a carcass. We realize the corpse is not worthy of us.

WEEDS

57
Jesus said,
"The Kingdom of the Father
is like a man with good seed.
His enemy came at night
and sowed weeds among the good seed.
The man did not allow the weeds to be pulled up;
he said,
'I am afraid you will pull up the wheat
along with the weeds.'
On the day of the harvest,
the weeds will be plainly visible,
and then they will be pulled up and burned."

What is this "Kingdom of the Father"? It is our consciousness, our awareness. "The Kingdom of Heaven is within you," said Jesus on another occasion.

Our consciousness is sown with seeds of both grain and weeds. Who is the enemy that comes "at night" (when we are not looking, when we are not awake, not aware) and scatters weed seed in our minds? It's us, of course. We do it ourselves all the time, through our attention. Attention energizes whatever it touches. Whatever we attend to, we become. We pay attention to the weed seeds in our psyches—our energetic beings—and they take root in us.

Once they are in there, says Jesus, they are not to be pulled out. Jesus' advice is to take out the weeds during the harvest, when we are gathering our crop, the fruitful yield of our consciousness.

And do you want to know the cosmic joke here? The so-called weeds are part of the harvest. Easily spotted, they provide energetic fuel. We are aflame with both the combustible nutrition of the grain and with the burning weeds. We are light and dark, seed and weed.

Of course, this is not easily or readily discerned when we insist on remaining at the particle level. We would rather fight the ongoing war of pulling the weeds out there in society . . . or in the devil . . . or in others . . . or even in some weak, punk image of ourselves. We want to be on the side of might and right. We divide ourselves in two and wrestle ourselves to the ground, choking our own throats.

It's painfully hilarious! I have to laugh at myself.

THE FINDING OF LIFE

58
Jesus said,
"Blessed is one who has labored
and found life."

Born out of the amniotic sac of the first birth, we take on the clothing or life of the human societal world, a world of customs and laws and imagery. Now we need a birthing labor of our own. We have not yet found life, although it is all around us. I do not speak here of just the "natural" world.

We must emerge from the human amniotic sac in which we are enfolded, this cultural conditioning and limitation of vision, this ignore-ance. This emerging is called labor because, like unhatched chicks, we have to peck at our own shells. When we persevere, we find life outside the shells of consciousness we solidified around ourselves so long ago.

The world rocks on—but it is no longer rocking us. We are, as Jesus says, blessed.

THE LIVING ONE

59
Jesus said,
"Look at the Living One while you are alive,
for if you die and then try to see him,
you won't be able to do so."

This human existence is a place of transition, an opportunity for transformation. To be born a human is a precious occurrence. The odds are small. Mister Buddha said it was about the same odds as a sea turtle in a boundless ocean surfacing once every gazillion years and its head popping into the hole of a single floating log on the entirety of the sea's surface.

We have to look at the Living One while we are in the flesh. This moment NOW is our opportunity.

Who is the Living One? Look and you will see.

THE PLACE
FOR REST

60
They saw a Samaritan going into Judea
carrying a lamb.
He asked his disciples,
"Why does that man carry the lamb around?"
They said to him, "So that he may kill it and eat it."
He said to them,
"While it is alive, he will not eat it,
but only when he has killed it
and it has become a corpse."
They said to him,
"He cannot do so otherwise."
He replied,
"You too should look for a place of rest
for yourselves,
lest you become a corpse and be eaten."

If you do not know your place of rest, how can I tell you?

Reflection will not do the job either. Caught in reflections, you are a corpse. Reflections are not the mirror.

When you know your mirror is a mirror, you will know your place of repose. Your place for rest is not a place. Your place for rest is no place.

The mirror knows it is a mirror but does not make itself into a mirror. This is the place for repose and rest. This is the Kingdom of Heaven spread out over the Earth. People are not aware of it, but it is pure awareness.

Awareness of awareness is already dead. We become corpses and are eaten.

THE SECOND BIRTH

61a
Jesus said,
"Two will lie on a bed.
One will die, and the other will live."

We know we are creatures of duality, of twoness. Our very bodies demonstrate this. We have "on the one hand" and "on the other hand." We look to "put our best foot forward." Our bodies are opposing halves with a centerline running down our middle.

We are also split in our thinking, which is composed of the continuous resolution of the ricochet between opposing forces: good-bad, right-wrong, us-them. We feel blessed relief when such cognitive dissonance is resolved.

A prime split in ourselves seems to be between our physical body (*soma*) and our energetic soul (*psyche*). At some point, the two will lie down on one bed. Only one will get up. The physical body will give way to the spiritual body.

We do not have to wait for physical death for this to occur.

WHO ARE YOU, MAN?

61b
Salome said to him,
"Who are you, man?
As though coming from someone,
you have sat on my couch
and eaten from my table."
Jesus answered her,
"I am he who exists from the One who is the same.
Some of the things of my Father
have been given to me."
Salome said, "I am your disciple."

Salome is referenced in Mark (16:1) as one of the three women who came to the tomb to anoint Jesus' body after the crucifixion. Evidently, she has invited Jesus and others over to her house for a meal. (At least one other person is present, who later records this conversation.)

They have finished eating when Salome asks an unusual question, one not generally asked of a dinner guest (but then Jesus was an unusual person): *Who are you, man?* Salome is still making up her mind about Jesus. She goes right to the heart of the matter: "Tell me with your own lips who you are."

When any of us is asked such a question, we generally respond with our name, our occupation, where we were born, what schools we went to, and so on. Superficial stuff. Not Jesus. He says: *I am he who exists from the One who is the same.* In other words, the one who is undivided, whose being is neither dualistic nor duel-istic.

Jesus speaks immediately of where he comes from: not the geographical but the spiritual location, his true source. He imparts some powerful information. He comes into being from somewhere else, from Someone else, and he is not only the same as the One he comes from, he comes from the One who is the same as Being, the One who is Undivided.

Some of the things of my Father have been given to me. Jesus is not a full presentation of his Source, but he does have many of his Source's characteristics. Only some of the things were given to him by the One who sired him. This is true for all of us who are embodyings of the Source.

Salome understands. With no hesitation she says: *I am your disciple.* "I am going to learn from you. I am going to embody the consciousness you embody. All the other concerns of life pale into insignificance."

THE INTERWHIRLING
AND THE DIVISIVE

61c
Jesus said to her,
"Therefore I say, the one who is undivided (unified),
will be filled with light,
but the one who is divided
will be filled with darkness."

When we are in that clear consciousness state of awareness—the state pointed to by the Buddhist term *sunyata* (emptiness, openness) and the Christian term *kenosis* (self-emptying)—walking between all stances and stancing, opening to the dances and the dancing, we are filled with light, the light that births us and sustains us. As Jesus said on more than one occasion: we are the light of the world.

Only when we split into two (right-wrong, good-bad, us-them, worthy-unworthy, human-not human . . . and so on, into infinity) do we become dark, sinister, subverting all to our split will. Plotting, planning, scheming are born. We fail to realize that we are making war on our own projected darkness.

When we claim our darkness, when we own the dark warrior—the Ninja's *noirior* within us—the twoness becomes a oneness.

This is a tough teaching and can be verified only through experience. We like to think we are champions of the right and good, on crusade against all unholy. We fear that if we give that up, we will be sunk, lost.

Instead we become more powerful. Nothing can stand against that which births us, breathes us, calls us into being. When we give up our divisiveness, when we surrender (are rendered, torn apart and put back together in an unpredictable, unimaginable form that has the Cosmos as both its center and its unfolding), we are an expression of the eternal ever-present Origin, the Wellspring of all existing.

Divisive consciousness is one of thesis and antithesis—and is never satisfied unless antithesis yields. Externally, that means: yield or die! Internally, that means we must surrender our own habits of stupor, greed, and hostility, against which ongoing war is waged.

Unified consciousness is one of synthesis, of claiming both thesis and antithesis on all levels and dimensions. The light of which Jesus speaks is the light that is inclusive of light-and-darkness. The *tai chi* (the boundless fist) becomes the *wu chi* (where yin and yang are indistinguishable), the state from which it sprang. With unified consciousness, the master warrior receives her graduation diploma: a silk with an empty circle.

And yet from a light-filled awareness, to speak of a unified consciousness and a divisive consciousness is a laughing matter.

Let me put it in four words, and then I'll shut up: mindful and relentless compassion.

THE TELLING OF THE MYSTERIES

62a
*Jesus said,
"I tell my mysteries
to those worthy of my mysteries."*

What are the mysteries? Who is worthy to be told them? Even if they are told, as Jesus frequently does, only "those who have ears" can hear. When we are full of ourselves—full of emotion, full of intellectual chitter-chatter—we cannot hear. We have to be silent before we can listen and be open in contemplation. Con-templum-ation: to sit quietly in the templum, the clear and open space for divining, for opening to the divine. Clear, open, capacious, expectant, attentive: only then are we worthy.

Worthiness comes too when we tire of abiding by social constructions of reality. We would rather listen to what the blood is singing . . . what the heart is radiating . . . what the Tao is Taoing. We are ready to listen to the great pulsations of the planet, the galaxies, the universe, the Cosmos, instead of the daily news. We make ourselves worthy by preparing an open space for the telling of the mysteries.

They will be told.

HANDIWORK

62b
*"Do not let your left hand
know what your right hand is doing."*

The endless conversations between the two sides of you are fruitless. Such a split-ness can go on forever. The self-argumentation of a split mind is valuable mainly as a sign of needed resolution.

When washing your hands, you do not know which hand is doing the washing. The washing is an interflow.

Come from your core, your center, and both hands are happy. Each performs its proper function while not wondering what the other is doing.

INVESTMENT

63

Jesus said,
"There was a rich man who had a lot of money.
He said, 'I'll invest my money,
so that I may sow, reap, plant,
and fill my storehouse with crops,
with then I'll lack nothing.'
Such were his intentions,
but that same night he died.
Let those who have ears hear."

We can invest in both material matter and in spiritual currency in order to feel secure. It is the "in order to" that does us in. No wrongness exists in either monetary or spiritual success.

Buddhist lore speaks of the spiritual seeker who floats off into an isolated pocket of self-satisfaction and remains there, believing he is snug and secure, that this state is nirvana. Once the self-blown bubble bursts, he has to come back to the point of bubble entry and start all over.

Jesus is pointing to the same phenomenon. For both types of security-seeking investor, death comes. Unexpectedly. This is a blessing, for the way they were pursuing security was false. Death is an ally; it removes all falsity. As Carlos Castaneda reminds us, death sits on our left shoulder and we should consult it in our plans and moves. Death is part of who we are, and it does not lie.

This is not only a reminder that "life is what happens when we are making other plans" . . . and that materialistic pursuits are like clothing a corpse with riches . . . and that no security exists but in the ephemeral. It is also a warning to those of us who amass spiritual wealth so as to ensure our place in the heavens, our resting place of comfort in the hereafter. We put our trust in the development of our own holosphere, a cosmic tomb.

It doesn't work that way. Give it all away all the time—and you will receive.

And we can't do it for that reason either.

THE STENCH
OF OUR OWN ARMPITS

64

*Jesus said,
"A man entertained guests.
And when he had prepared the dinner,
he sent his servant to invite his guests.
The servant went to the first one and said to him,
'My master invites you.'
He replied, 'I have claims against some merchants.
They are coming to me this evening.
I must go do business with them.
I ask to be excused from the dinner.'
The servant went to another and said,
'My master has invited you.'
He answered,
'I have just bought a house
and am required for the day.
I won't have any spare time.'*

The servant went to another and said to him,
'My master invites you.'
He replied, 'My friend is going to get married,
and I have to prepare the banquet.
I won't be able to come.
I ask to be excused from the dinner.'
The servant went to another and said,
'My master invites you.'
He answered, 'I have just bought a farm,
and I'm on my way to collect the rent.
I won't be able to come. I ask to be excused.'
The servant returned and said to his master,
'Those whom you invited to the dinner
have asked to be excused.'
The master said to his servant,
'Go outside to the streets
and invite anyone you can find to the dinner.'
Businesspeople and merchants
will not enter the places of my Father."

Jesus must have experienced this himself. His life consisted of inviting people to a feast for the soul, to food that would energize the spirit, that would produce satisfaction, happiness, and joy. Like today, though, folk were too busy with the agenda of their own mindset to be open to such food.

We are too busy buying and selling our own aura, too busy smelling our own armpits and calling the scent wonderful. We do not know how much we love our own smell. We wish to sell our body odor to the entire world. This is our busyness. We are merchants and salesmen of our own stench.

We are too busy to open ourselves to the Awareness that Jesus experiences and teaches, the places of the Father. We have no room in the "In." The invitation then goes instead to those out in the streets, those not caught in the constrictive mindsets of self-love (and self-hate, its shadow twin), those who have at least semi-permeable membranes for brains.

We receive great Awareness according to our capacity. And capaciousness is a function of letting go, not a busy-busy gathering together.

TENANT
FARMERS

65
He said,
"A good man owned a vineyard.
He leased it to tenant farmers
so that they would work it
and he could collect the produce from them.
He sent his servant so that the tenants
would give him the produce.
They seized his servant
and beat him nearly to death.
The servant went back and told his master.
The master said, 'Maybe they didn't recognize him.'
He sent another servant.
The tenants beat this one as well.
Then the owner sent his son and said,
'Perhaps they will show respect to my son.'
Because the tenants knew that it was he

who was the heir to the vineyard,
they seized him and killed him.
Whoever has ears, hear!"

We live on the plane of the horizontal and ignore the vertical. We are dirt and water walking around, wishing to claim it all, forgetting that we did not make ourselves. The vertical descends from above and ascends from below to claim its portion. We kill that part of our souls. We keep killing it every time it makes its appearance. This is spiritual suicide. We are tenant farmers, and the rent will come due. Though we kill the urges of the spirit within us, the owner of the vineyard will have the last say.

CHOOSING THE CORNERSTONE

66
Jesus said,
"Show me the stone that the builders rejected.
It is the cornerstone."

A building's cornerstone is important. Its size and shape and weight set the tone for the structure of the entire building. Builders take great care in selecting their cornerstones.

Conventional theological thinking has it that Jesus is the rejected cornerstone upon which the Christian church is built. Existing church structures seek to maintain their legitimacy by claiming this verse.

I do not see Jesus forecasting here the existence of the Roman Orthodox, the Greek Orthodox, the Russian Orthodox, and the thousands of Protestant Orthodox churches. At the time this conversation takes place, he is talking with his disciples who are concerned with the spiritual and political situation of the day, much as we are now. The stone that the builders of that society selected as their cornerstone was the choice plump one, the one that satisfied greed and lust for power.

With his emphasis on this saying (which comes from Psalm 118), Jesus is turning the world inside out, making the invisible world visible. The power-greed-fame world's cornerstone is not the one on which to build. Instead, we must build on the stone the world rejects.

Each of us chooses the cornerstone on which to build our lives. Separative consciousness chooses the instant gratification of physical materiality. Unitive consciousness chooses the Source, the Wellspring, the One-Who-Breathes-Us as its cornerstone.

Jesus recommends the generally rejected one.

THE EXTERNAL
AND THE INTERNAL
ARE ONE-TERNAL

67
Jesus said,
"If you know everything else,
but do not know yourself,
you know nothing."

Jesus points to two realms here: the realm of the self and the realm of everything else. A higher, more inclusive view sees this as an arbitrary distinction, yet one that most everyone makes. There is "me" and there is "everything else." This is a dualistic, duelistic world we create for ourselves.

We can focus outwardly and know everything about everything, be capable of expressing an opinion on any topic: politics, religion, social issues, computer systems, astronomy, cosmology, the Oscars, genetically modified foods, relatives, sexual preferences. . . . Everything!

We appear very wise and knowledgeable. But Jesus says if we do not know ourselves, we know nothing. If our light of awareness is not turned inward and our own consciousness illuminated, we know nothing. The Kingdom of Heaven is not "out there" but within.

When we sit quietly and listen to all our inner voices, look at all our inner images, taste all our inner tastes—without clinging to any aspect of this inner universe—we eventually settle into the Wellspring producing all that springs forth. We grow calm, quiet, aware, present, fearless, open, loving. We see and know that the internal and the external are not divided but are one Flow.

Now we know that knowing "everything else" is knowing nothing . . . and knowing ourselves is knowing everything.

THE HEALING
OF BLESSING

68
*Jesus said,
"Blessed are you
when you are hated and persecuted.
No place will be found where they persecuted you."*

Think of blessing as a light filling your entire being. Light flows through you, healing all impurity. Jesus says that when hate comes your way, be filled with blessing. Hatred and persecution can find no place to enter. If you look for any sign of it, any spot where it resides, you will find nothing, no place.

The best way to do this is to be filled with blessing all the time, persecution or not. Why wait until hatred comes? Be filled with blessing now.

THE SELF-PURSUIT OF PERSECUTION

69a
Jesus said,
"Blessed are those who have been persecuted within themselves.
They have truly come to know the Father."

Jesus is putting some high praise on a certain group of folk here. He is saying they are blessed: consecrated, set aside, made holy, given great happiness. Because of certain actions and the result of those actions, they have found a space called blessed. They have *really* come to *know* the Source of all being, the Wellspring of existence.

How is this possible? The answer is startling, unexpected: it is possible because they "have been persecuted within themselves." To persecute means to continually harass someone in such a manner as to cause her to suffer. First of all, note the past tense in what Jesus says: the persecution is over. Those of us who are being persecuted within ourselves right now are not blessed. That should be immediately obvious.

Who or what did that persecuting within itself? It was once the fashion (and still is among some) to objectify it (turn it into an object) and say it was the devil or imps from hell that did the persecuting. But no: it is you. It is you continually harassing yourself and causing your own suffering.

Am I good enough? Do I measure up? What if all my plans fail? What if this happens or that happens? What is this zit upon my soul? What did so-and-so mean by that? Will I have enough to retire? Why don't my children straighten out? Why don't I have a more beautiful body? How come I can't kick this habit? Why am I so bored all the time? Why am I so tired all the time? Why don't other people treat me in the sublime way I should be treated? And on and on and on . . . I I I I I!

Persecution is self-reflection: split off from the flow of life and staring into a self-made mirror. The persecution is over when we open and continue opening to a wider awareness than Oh-So-Low-Me-Oh!

Jesus tells us how to do this: We *truly come to know the Father*. We come to know the Source of all being by whatever name (and the Source has many names). To really know means to become-as-one-with. We are the Wellspring springing. We are the Source sourcing. We are the Father fathering. We are the Mother mothering. We are Wisdom wisdoming. We are the Universe universing.

When we know that—*really* know that—all persecution within ourselves is over. We are blessed.

GETTING A BELLY FULL

69b
*"Blessed are those who go hungry,
in order to fill the bellies of the needy."*

Blessedness is a state of radiant content, "content" both in the adjective sense of relaxed and satisfied ease and in the noun sense of what fills something. When we empty ourselves so as to fill others, there are no others. There exists only blessedness, only a gentle powerful radiance with no bounds.

We are hungry in the sense we are doing without food for the ego: no nutriment for an encapsulated, separate self. We are now fed by universal rather than a personal energy, by the springing of the Wellspring rather than the dead waters of ingrown reflection.

All around us benefit. All who come in contact with this blessedness will receive. They will have their bellies filled, according to their capacity.

Our spiritual hunger dissolves the sense of separate self. This dissolution of separation allows us to be food for the needy, for those who are spiritually hungry. The vital energies of the Life Force reverberate without end. This is blessedness.

GERMINATION

70
Jesus said,
"If you give rise to that which is within you,
what you have will save you.
If you do not give rise to it,
what you do not have will destroy you."

A seed has the mystery of nothingness at its core. It is this nothingness opening to the rhythms of light and dark and water and drought that is its "germ" (that which produces its germination). When the seed gives rise to this, it is saved. It becomes the unique plant it is, one like no other.

If the seed does not give rise to its germ of nothingness, it will have no germination. What it does not have destroys it.

As the seed is, so are we.

These words came to me so long ago, clearly and distinctly: "Sit in the seat at the center of your soul." This is essential for growth, for growing into the being that we are capable of being. When we operate from this seat at the center of our souls—from our cores—we flourish. We are saved.

When we do not—when we operate instead from our peripheral beings, from our fantasy selves, or from the three stooges (anger, greed, stupor)—we are not growing from our cores. We will not germinate as the unique beings that we are. What we do not have will destroy us.

We cannot effectively plan our own salvation, our own germination. We have to "grow" it, from inside out. When we give rise to that which is within us, nothing outside us can stop us. We become the beautiful souls we already are.

"I"
AND "NO ONE"

71
Jesus said,
"I will destroy this house,
and no one will be able to build it again."

I interpret this saying as if it were a Zen koan. You may object. Especially if you are a learned scholar who wishes to stay in the worldview you imagine Jesus maintained at the time. Jesus, however, destroys all worldviews, all shells in which we wish to remain hidden.

I will destroy this house. The "I" that we are will destroy our house of personality, of character, and of soul. The "I" is a fig leaf of our imagination that attempts to cover the nakedness of our souls—but it will never stretch far enough to do so. "I" has its own will: the will to destroy the souls we are.

No one will be able to build it again. No one; "the name that can be named is not the eternal name," says the Tao Te Ching. The Wellspring, our Source, The-One-Who-Breathes-Us cannot be captured in a name.

Meister Eckhart and others did their best to speak to this by saying, "God is a circle with no circumference whose center is everywhere." God is a Zero without the O. God is the Fertile Void out of which all things spring. God is not even one. God is no one.

And it is No One who will be able to build it again. It is our Source who repairs the damage the "I" has done. This is called forgiveness.

It is always happening, right now.

A TEACHING MOMENT

72

A man said to him,
"Tell my brothers
to divide my father's possessions with me."
Jesus replied,
"Man, who made me a divider?"
He turned to his disciples and asked them,
"Really, am I a divider?"

Jesus' words here have been interpreted as being sarcasm, not so much because of his reply to the man wanting Jesus' persuasive power to work in his behalf, but because of Jesus' remark to his disciples, as if this is an inside joke Jesus and his disciples will laugh at together, leaving the questioner shut out and embarrassed. I do not see this as consistent with Jesus' way of being.

My intuition is that the man seeking resolution of this domestic dispute had first approached one or more of the disciples.

Since they don't know what to say to him, they tell him to ask Jesus for help. Jesus' reply ("Man, who made me a divider?") shows that Jesus is immediately aware of the inadequacy of his disciples' understanding.

This dialogue is not between Jesus and the man who felt wronged, but between Jesus and his disciples. First, he wonders aloud who made him a divider, which may have set off some nervousness among those who did see him that way. Jesus taught unification, not division. (Saying 61c: *The one who is unified will be filled with light, but the one who is divided will be filled with darkness.*)

Then Jesus focuses full attention on his disciples (those who accepted his discipline) with a strong and true teaching question, the best kind of question, one they have to answer themselves: *Really, am I a divider?*

The very question itself shows that Jesus was not trying to make fun of the man by dividing him from the disciples as an ignorant man not in the know with the "in" crowd. The question was designed to get the disciples to think and to understand.

MOVING WITH THE RADIANCE

73

Jesus said,
"The harvest is great,
but the workers are few.
Ask the master of the harvest
to send more workers."

A harvest is potential food, nurturance. As such, it is worthless unless it is gathered. Workers are needed.

The harvest is the potential for the expansion of human consciousness. We need more workers to gather in this potential, to make it part of ourselves, to dissolve our bounds and go beyond.

This is the task for each of us. To ask the master to send more workers is to energize ourselves. What are we doing to contribute to the evolution of human consciousness? We do not just hang out until we die and then evolve. Our opportunity is now. Jesus knows this.

Ancient wisdom has it that God—our Source, our Origin—is a self-sacrificing, slow-motion explosion radiating outward in all directions . . . and that we are the frontier of that radiance. We either move with the radiance or we move against it.

A worker for the harvest moves with it.

NOBODY IN THE WELL

74
He said,
"Master, there are many around the drinking barrel,
but there is nobody in the well."

The spirit of this age consists both of inertia/stupor (we wish to make no move except to our next entertainment) and frenetic activity on the horizontal plane. Though we know we need to descend into our spiritual depths, we are hesitant, unwilling to do so.

We continue to oscillate between stupor and restless activity, half-hoping that someone else will bring us spiritual water to drink, water that impels us to go beyond the rigid bounds that mummify us in our self-created tombs of desiccation.

We must climb into the Well ourselves. We have to stop standing around the drinking barrel and take the leap. No one else can do it for us. And NOW is the only time there is.

STANDING AT THE THRESHOLD

75

Jesus said,
"Many are standing at the door,
but only the single will enter the bridal chamber."

Ah, yes! The bridal chamber, the alchemical furnace in which we are transformed from leaden creatures into golden spirits. Many stand at the door, peeking in, studying it, thinking about it, hesitating, yearning in their hearts . . . but with their cold feet frozen to the spot.

What's my problem? Why do I not transform? Sex, drugs, rock and roll? Pride, fear, anger? Ignore-ance, stupor-idity? Lover of the human-created? Forget all that. Pluck off those leeches. Otherwise, I won't make it through the bridal chamber's security gate. Alarms will ring: "He is not single!"

To be transformed, I gotta give it all up. Surrender is the hardest thing. But one gets back ten zillion fold. Can't do it for that, though; that's definitely un-single. The alchemical furnace with its fires of transformation is entered alone!

Can I do it?

THE PEARL

76a
Jesus said,
"The Kingdom of the Father is like a merchant
who had a consignment of goods to sell
who then found a pearl.
The merchant was a thinking man.
He sold the merchandise
and bought the pearl for himself."

The pearl was more valuable to the man than his merchandise. Merchandise comes and goes; the pearl is to keep. The pearl comes with a price, however.

Jesus says the man "found" a pearl. We might think that means he stumbled upon it, and thus it automatically was his. No. He had to rid himself of what was less valuable to obtain what was most valuable. He did not do this spontaneously. He thought about it. Then, after coming to a decision, *he sold the merchandise and bought the pearl for himself.*

What is the pearl? What is this that is of more value than anything else?

Our own souls.

And yet we can see that our souls are not our own. They are bought with a price. A price has already been paid by the One who brings our soul into existence. Now it is our turn to also pay a price. Our souls are price-worthy: precious.

The steps are simple:

1. We see the preciousness of our souls, of the souls we are.
2. We give up all we possess, all we cling to, in order to have them.

Would you "gain the whole world and lose your own soul"?

TREASURE

76b
*"You too should seek
for enduring treasures that no moth can eat
and no worm destroy."*

We are continuously inhaling from and exhaling into the Divine. We are being breathed, though we ignore this great treasure, preferring instead to scamper around in our latest escapades and incessant melodramas.

We are not to identify with the breathing animal we are, as magnificent and wondrous as it is. Instead, we breathe in from and out into the eternal Halation (hale: hearty, whole, holy), That which breathes all. We will have a final exhalation. Then we will follow this last breathing out—our final exhale—to the place and treasure of the Mystery that breathes us.

We are this breathing. We are the rhythmic tide of the Divine.

Jesus brings us good tidings.

HOLOARCHY

77a
Jesus said,
"I am the light that is above everything.
I am everything.
Everything comes forth from me
and to me everything reaches."

It's pretty simple really. We are made up of elements of the universe, of the Cosmos. We are made of earth, earth is made of stars, and so on, back to the primal material and that which produced it.

Some of us are more consciously aware of this than others. "Aware" does not mean intellectual understanding alone. It means an experiencing, an awareness-ing. We feel and know we are the universe embodying.

Jesus knows this. *I am the light that is above everything.* He is the Light that birthed and births all living. In this sentence, Jesus speaks in hierarchical terms; the light is above everything. In other places, he refers to the light within: the light proceeds from inside out.

I am everything. At our deepest and highest realms, *we* are everything. We breathe the breath of all life living with no separation.

Everything comes forth from me and to me everything reaches. The flow of life is reciprocal. That which breathes out life breathes in life. This is the cry of mystics and mythopoets of all religions and spiritual paths across the ages: *Tat tvam asi.* Thou art that.

When opening awareness beyond our particularity, we know along with Jesus that we are the light, that we are everything. Through the grace of life, we belong to the family of that which births everything and to which all returns.

SPLIT AND LIFT

77b
*"Split a piece of wood, and I am there.
Lift up a stone,
and you will find me there."*

Jesus is an embodying of the Life Force (as we all are). He gives flesh to the sacrificial outbreathing that births all that is. Not all of us are aware that we are personifications of the Life Force, but Jesus is. Thus, he can make this statement.

The Cosmos is a vibrational flow of energy assuming many forms. The forms we see depend primarily on our perception: what we have been taught to see and what we allow ourselves to see.

The universe you are "in" is you looking back at you.

The great I Am is everywhere.

THE DESERT PLACE

78
Jesus asked,
"Why have you come out into the desert?
To see a reed shaken by the wind?
To see a man clothed in fine garments
like your kings and your great men?
They wear fine garments
and cannot understand truth."

When we go into our desert place—our quiet place away from the turmoil—why do we go there? When we retreat into meditation or prayer, what are our expectations? What do we expect to see?

Our expectations color our experience. Do we expect to see ourselves as reeds shaken by the winds of Spirit? Then we might as well get up and go on our way. We reek of self-fulfillment.

Do we expect to see ourselves clothed in elegant spiritual garments? To sit inside a spiritual bubble of refined purity removed from the world? That bubble will eventually burst. Until then, we will be insufferable, with an air, however slight, of superiority. We reek of smugness. *We wear fine garments and cannot understand the truth.*

In today's world, it is essential to open ourselves to a quiet inner space. The question here is: Why do we go there? A worthy answer is: For no reason, no reason at all. When we are shorn of all expectation, then we know and are the truth.

THE WOMB
AND THE BREASTS

79

A woman from the crowd said to him,
"Blessed are the womb that bore you
and the breasts that nourished you."
He replied,
"Blessed are those who have heard
the word of the Father and really kept it.
For there will be days when you will say,
'Blessed are the womb that has never conceived
and the breasts that have never given milk.'"

This triplet—the three sentences above—has this form: affirmation, Greater Affirmation, negation, leading to openness (+ + − = 0).

A woman from the crowd: She is an individual. Rilke has pointed out that God does not love crowds. Crowds are thin soup compared to the rich relationship of the individual heart with the Beloved. Rumi backs this up.

The woman gives Jesus what can, in a one-dimensional realm, be considered to be a strong compliment. But Jesus does not flush with pleasure. Nor does he offer a socially polite, "Thank you."

Instead, Jesus responds from a more powerfully inclusive dimension, from the consciousness he embodies and by which he lives: *Blessed are those who have heard the word of the Father and really kept it.* This is the true blessedness. In every moment, we open to "the word of the Father," to our Source sourcing, to the Wellspring of our springing, and embody that word, that wording.

Jesus then points out to the woman that while caught in the flush of enthusiasm now, at some point (in days to come), she will change her mind. She will move from affirmation to negation, from + to –. This is the way of humans.

He pointed her (and us) to the true way, to stay open (0) to the word that has been spoken since the beginning, that is spoken even now, the word at the core of our hearts, the word that speaks our truth if we but listen. This is the true womb and the true breasts of nourishment.

THE BODY
OF THE WORLD

80
Jesus said,
"Whoever has come to know the world
has found the body.
The world is not worthy
of whoever has found the body."

We are born into the world. What is the world? Is it rocks and sticks and water? Is it flowers and birds and air? Is it a child's laughter? Is it sweat and blood and tears? Is it job and family and home?

The world appears as all this and more. The key word here is *appears*. Beneath the appearance, the world is a dynamic interflow of energy exchange. All is in relation to all. Indra's net is a useful metaphor: a cosmic net with a jewel at each interstice reflecting all the other jewels. Each component of the world reflects—is called into existence by—all other components. Each component is a microcosm of the all.

When we know this, we have found the body of the world. The body of the world is interwhirling energy producing distinctions that are not distinct. Within that is a fertile emptiness we can only begin to comprehend. Or rather, It comprehends us.

When we have found that body, when we know we are that body, the apparitional world is not worthy of us. We are not worthy when we walk through life attending to only the superficial appearance. We need to come to know the world, to find its body. Then we are worthy of the world. We are its body.

RICHNESS

81
Jesus said,
"Let the person who has become rich be the ruler.
Let the one who has power renounce it."

This does *not* mean whoever has a lot of money should rule. Having a lot of money does not make you rich. Richness is of the heart, the soul. Nothing that stays here when you die is of any richness. Your richness is the warm and brilliant radiance of connection with your angel, your higher being already on the other shore. With this merging, you now rule.

Nor is richness based on a rule of laws and force and power (power is a trap that drains the soul). It is a radiance of spirit that can never be overcome.

FIRE IN THE WHOLE!

82

Jesus said,
"Whoever is near me is near the fire.
Whoever is far from me is far from the Kingdom."

Fire represents great intensity. Jesus burns with intensity, with spirit. He is in tune with the elemental forces of transformation.

Think of the alchemical furnace, the furnace in which base metal is transformed to gold, all impurities burned away. As a representative of that alchemical Fire, as the Fire Itself, Jesus gives us a warning sign: *Whoever is near me is near the fire.* If you don't want transformation and its accompanying pain and loss, do not come near. Stay over there, far from the Reality more powerful than the human-created world.

When we hang out with the Wholly One, our spirits are aflame.

Orthodoxy identifies fire with hell. Once again Jesus turns things inside out and upside down.

HIDDEN AND REVEALED

83

Jesus said,
"The images are revealed to people,
but the light in them remains hidden
in the image of the light of the Father.
He will be revealed,
but his image will remain hidden by his light."

Four words stand out here: *Revealed. Hidden. Revealed. Hidden.* Think of a light blinking on and off. This is the nature of these images, the powerful symbols that show us the essence of life, of being.

Revelation comes. We think we've got it. Like Peter at the Transfiguration, we want to build an altar there, a church, a society, a form. We want to stop.

No. Something is hidden within the revelation. Something more. Something deeper. We press on with no clinging.

Ah! Revealed! We understand more. We see the image of the Father's light, our Source's light within the first revelation. He is in there somewhere. Hidden.

We catch a glimpse! Revealed! Our souls are thrilled. Then the glimpse gives way abruptly to the darkness of greater light. We begin to understand. We stop looking out there. He is in here looking out. He is the light within. We have him cornered now.

Blink! He is inside. He is outside. He is neither inside nor outside. He is both inside and outside. Inside and outside are one and the same.

Only light remains.

YOUR ORIGINAL FACE

84
Jesus said,
"When you see your likeness, you are pleased.
But when you see your images,
which came into being before you,
and which are immortal and invisible,
how much can you bear?"

"What was your original face before your mother and father were born?" (Hui-neng)

Can you see your face before you were born, "your images that came into being before you did"? Jesus says you can. But can you bear it?

We like to reflect upon ourselves in our current state. We are captivated by our images in mirrors, in store windows. We sigh. We like this. We don't like that. But generally, we are pleased when we see our own likenesses.

What about the images of ourselves before we were born, the images that never die, the images that are invisible to the fleshly eye? Do we like to reflect upon those? Have we even stopped to acknowledge their existence?

Can you see yourself as an explosion of chaotically creative energy forever unfolding? Can you see yourself as walking with God in the cool of the evening? Can you see yourself as the fearsome fangs of eternal death?

What was your original face before your mother and father were born? Can you look the Source smack dab in the face and live? Do you dare? Will your pitiful little self-image be burned to a cinder?

How much can you bear?

WORTHY

85

Jesus said,
"Adam came into being from great power and wealth,
but he did not become worthy of you.
For had he been worthy of you
he would not have experienced death."

Jesus is telling us of our worth.

But worthy to whom?

Worthy to ourselves in realizing who we are, not just suckling babes crawling on a planet seeking what we may devour, not just unique creations arising from the Ground of Existence and then, after a few short years, dissolving—but immortal manifestations of our Father, our Source.

Worthy to God, our Father and our Mother, the Wellspring of which we are the offspring. We are loved, and when we love in return, a circuit is completed that is never broken.

NO PLACE

86

Jesus said,
"Foxes have their holes, and birds have their nests,
but the Son of Man has no place
to lay his head down and rest."

For those of us who follow the path that Jesus walked, there is no place to lay down our heads and rest. What is this path? It is the path of the "Son of Man" (gender is not an issue here, for the Son of Man is the child of humanity), the path of those who are evolving beyond ordinary consciousness. The offspring of humanity is a further developing of humankind, a birthing beyond human. Ordinary consciousness opens to integral consciousness.

As this transition occurs, we find we have no place to lay down our heads and rest. There is no doctrinal matrix, no set of rules of worship, no formula to follow, no ritual. While others may find comfort in these forms, we have moved on down the road. All falls away, and we are standing now transparent and open in a full-disclosure cosmos. Nothing is hidden. Our awareness continues to open.

To lay our heads down in a hole or nest is death to a child of humanity, to one who has moved on. That is why rituals and creeds have lost meaning and are no longer necessary. When we open ourselves to participation in the Cosmos—*as* the Cosmos—we do not look back. Once the goose in the old Buddhist koan has escaped the bottle, it does not turn around and try to fit itself back in.

If Jesus visited a church on communion Sunday, would he drink his blood and eat his flesh? I doubt it. I think he would say: "Enough already! Quit toasting my demise and resurrection! Stop slamming down shots of my blood! Cease munching on dry wafers of discontent! Get off your butts and out into the street! The time has come! Stop drifting off into some realm of spiritual euphoria! Wake up! I'm here!"

The child of humanity has no place to lay down her head and rest. Once we go through a door, we have no reason to go through it again and again. We do not become attached to the door, no matter how sacred or holy it appears. Instead, we move through to the other side, to the next room. And we don't build a nest *there* either. There's no need. The nest for the child of humanity is a sphere with infinity in every "direction." Our nest is the eternal ever-expanding Cosmos of radiance, grace, and mercy (combined with a strong sense of loving humor).

We are at home . . . so we need no home.

WRETCHED

87
Jesus said,
"Wretched is the body that is depending on a body,
and wretched is the soul depending on these two."

"To retch" is to vomit. The root word means "to expel." The root word of wretched means "an exile." Combined, they give us a good understanding of what it means to be wretched. And just as we think we have reached a new low in our wretchedness, we plummet to an even lower state of misery. We have vomited ourselves.

Jesus generally speaks in response to practical situations. This saying can be read as his heartfelt response to any of us as we grow older and eventually must depend upon the care of others. "Wretched is a body depending on a body." This dependence can of course also take place when we are sick or disabled in other ways than advanced age. When that happens, for whatever reason, we are no longer in charge; we are no longer in control. The interplay between humility (humiliation) and that spark of independent self-reliance that always burns within us creates the conflict known as wretchedness.

Jesus was always pointing to higher, wider, deeper realms beyond the everyday grind of the body. To whomever he is speaking in this saying (I imagine it is a confined person in one of the households he's visiting), he immediately shifts from body to soul. "Wretched is a soul depending on these two."

As a healer, Jesus gives the prescription for the way out of the wretchedness: Stop depending on the body depending on a body. Move to the soul level. This is true for us all. Each of us traps ourselves in being a body depending on a body. In that sense, every one of us is sick and disabled. In this saying, Jesus points to the cure.

Even more deeply, we are wretched when we fashion an image of a body upon which we depend . . . and then look at that body with a second body we mentally and emotionally create, thereby seeing ourselves in our own eyes. These are the two bodies at the beginning of an endless hall of mirrors, in which we go through life (rather than *as* life), never opening as the souls we are, forever wretchedly depending on these two.

And we call this rational!

THE MESSENGERS

88

Jesus said,
"The messengers and the prophets will come to you,
and they will give you what belongs to you.
You in turn should give them what you have,
and say to yourselves,
'When will they come and take what is theirs?'"

They are coming. They are on the way. And they are here. The messengers. The prophets. Where are they? They are deep inside us when we drop away all the foo-foo, all the paraphernalia we carry, when we stop playing the dung beetle pushing its precious ball of anal waste.

The messengers are coming to us with the prophets, and they will give us what is properly ours. This is exciting—and also a little frightening. Especially if we feel we already have what is properly ours, our internal and external accumulations we have struggled so hard to amass: the dung balls we regard so highly.

No one's shit smells so good as my own.

And they will give you what belongs to you. Why, the presumption! How can we trust them? We are rational beings raised in the tradition of Plato and Aristotle, upon which Western culture and its advanced shrivelization are based! (I am reminded of a quote here from Peter Kingsley's *Reality*: "Rationality is simply mysticism misunderstood.")

We say we want to change, but we hesitate when change is right at our door. Do we dare accept what is properly ours, sight unseen? Is life that ambiguous, that uncertain, that unknown?

But wait! There's more! Not only should we then give them what we have—they are going to take what is theirs. Even more distressing for us Cling-ons!

O Lord, I will be stripped. Totally stripped of all I have thought myself to be. Opening to the messengers and the prophets. No longer relying on the human world.

Transformation: We let go of what we have. They take what is theirs. They give us what is properly ours.

How do we make sense of this? We don't. We experience it.

THE CUP

89

Jesus said,
"Why do you wash the outside of the cup?
Don't you realize that the one who made the inside
also made the outside?"

The inside of the cup is empty. It is the formless. The outside of the cup is its form. Both are essential. The formless and the form, the inside and the outside, have an intimate working relationship. Each births the other. Their difference is only a working of our minds. A fine working, to be sure, a working of distinction.

Why do you wash the outside of the cup? Why give all the attention to the form? To trap ourselves in the world of appearance is to ignore what gives rise to appearance. To pay attention to the form so we can neglect the formless is a one-dimensional love affair. Our love (the washing) stops short at the superficial.

When we open ourselves to both formless and form as one, we are engaged in whole-cup washing.

Here is a koan: *What is the sound of whole-cup washing?*

GENTLENESS AND REST

90
Jesus said,
"Come to me.
My yoke is easy.
My leadership is gentle.
You will find rest for yourselves."

When a great consciousness is born into this world, spiritual paths are founded upon the influential radiance of that consciousness. It arouses both antagonism and joy. Its influence reverberates across time and through space. Jesus is such a consciousness.

Here he stands and looks at ordinary human consciousness: caught up, entangled, ensnared in emotional turmoil, cognitive chatter, false imaginings. His heart opens with love, with compassion.

"Come to me," he says. "Let me share my consciousness with you, the awareness of a realm including and beyond that of the physical senses." A realm in which we are always already home. The realm out of which we were born, where we now dwell (though we may not see it or we catch only glimpses of it), and to which we will return.

"Shift consciousness," Jesus says. Be born out of ordinary awareness into the supra-ordinal, into integral awareness, into awareness of the vast and personal interflow of spirit and spiritual beings.

The yoke of which Jesus speaks here is the wooden collar put on the neck of oxen to allow them to put their shoulders into a load and pull it more easily. Jesus uses this as he did other examples from daily life to illustrate his point. Folks know what he's talking about.

Jesus says his yoke is easy, and in another saying similar to this one, he said his burden was light. I envision the stubborn ox I am whose burden has been transformed to Light. The yoke I formerly wore, the yoke of human fear and anger, has vanished. I wear a yoke so easy there is no yoke at all.

All the great consciousnesses tell us this. Drop the little isolated protoplasmic blob consciousness and open to a wider, deeper, greater Reality.

As Mister Bobby Dylan said, "You gotta serve somebody." We either serve our ego power—the constricted, self-kissing, other-scorning, but-what-about-me? consciousness—or we serve the Larger Self we are. We remain in ordinary consciousness or we open to universal consciousness. Christ consciousness is a portal to that realm.

TELL US
WHO YOU ARE

91
They said to him,
"Tell us who you are
so that we can believe in you."
He replied,
"You read the face of the sky and the earth,
but you don't recognize the one
who is right in front of you.
You don't know how to read this moment."

Though the disciples are in Jesus' immediate presence, they are also in the same situation as we are: they are trying to make sense of what's going on while living it out.

Like all humans, they want to believe in something. They want some sort of foundation on which to stand. In this saying, they are doing their best to make Jesus create that for them.

Tell us who you are so that we can believe in you. We humans so want to be told. Despite our independent streaks, we are little fascists underneath it all. We want some authority over us. We want a club, an organization, a union. We want a creed, a gavel to call the meeting to order, and someone to wield it. We want to believe *together* and sing our marching song.

Tell us who you are so that we can believe in you. Some of them already have the answer they wanted to hear. If Jesus didn't give them that, so much the worse for Jesus. They will be on their way regardless. Others have already devoted themselves to him and are wishing for more cognitive understanding. They eagerly await his words.

Once they've asked their question, you can bet that all eyes and ears are fixated on Jesus. And he immediately turns their attention away from him. *You read the face of the sky and the earth, but you don't recognize the one who is right in front of you. You don't know how to read this moment.* He is not looking to found a Jesus cult. He shifts attention to the sky and to the earth. He says we humans are looking way up there and way down here. And in our looking, we are fixated only on appearance—the casting of our own images, our own imagery, on the world around us, rather than letting the world—the Cosmos—disclose itself to us. We are blinded by our own light.

In this blindness, we do not recognize what is right in front of us. We are too busy scurrying to the next thing, living in what our minds have conjured. And when we get to the next thing, we are not there either. We are perpetually leaning into some imagined future. At the time of death, we will perhaps realize that we have never fully lived. We don't know the nature of the present time, the quality of this moment *now*, the only moment in which we truly exist.

Nor do we know the nature of the present time in the sense of our continuously being born while continuously passing away. Like waves in the ocean, we seem to have continuity of existence, but we are always different from what we were. We are embodyings of new water from the Source.

ASK

92
Jesus said,
"Seek and you will find."
He said,
"In the past I did not answer your questions.
Now I am willing to answer,
but you don't ask."

Wisdom surrounds us. It infuses us with its clarity and depth of understanding if we but allow it. Superseding rational understanding, it comes only through our naked openness and our asking.

We are fortunate to be born as humans, with human consciousness and awareness. Such a birth is not to be taken for granted. It is a birth of potential transformation. But if the conduit that we are is clogged with our clinging to our own hubbub, no Wisdom comes. If I only have eyes for me, my third eye does not open.

Jesus, representing this Wisdom, says to someone long ago: *I am willing to answer, but you don't ask*. This is still the case. Universal Wisdom is open to us, but only if we open to It.

The method for doing so is well known: Sit down and let go. Let go of mind chatter. Let go of emotional surges. Let go of fear. Let go of anger. Let go of boredom. Let go of itches. Let go of scratching. Let go of melodrama. Let go of hunger. Let go of thirst. Let go of letting go.

When we are calm and expectantly open, Wisdom comes. No bounds exist between us and the Wisdom of the One-Who-Breathes-Us. This Wisdom often cannot be put into words. It is a knowing.

As he speaks this saying, I imagine Jesus is with one or more persons who are silent in his presence. Not the silence of contented togetherness, but a silence of sealed-off confusion. Ever-mindful of every situation, Jesus calls them on it: "Wisdom is here with you. Ask."

DISCLOSURE OF THE HOLY

93
Jesus said,
"Do not give what is holy to dogs,
lest they carry it off to the dung heap.
Do not throw pearls to pigs,
for they might. . ."

We cannot share the depths of our beings with those who cannot hear and understand. Nor should we attempt to do so. The sacred becomes cheapened.

Disclose yourself to those with an affinity of soul. Then your treasure—your "holy things"—will be amplified and strengthened.

Do not blaspheme and let the dog and pig part of you invade and loot your inner sanctuary. You will find yourself on the dung heap and torn apart.

FINDING AND OPENING

94
Jesus said,
"Whoever seeks will find.
Whoever knocks,
it will be opened."

This is the kept promise of the Cosmos. Awareness continues to open as attention keeps knocking on the door. What door? The thin permeable membrane that separates our consciousness from the larger consciousness, our awareness from great awareness.

How do we knock? By opening to the highest, widest, deepest awareness we can muster. We push the bounds of our consciousness. We do this through contemplation: con-templum-ation, going to the templum—the clear and open space inside—where knowledge and understanding, grace and love are received.

We knock, not with agitated fervor but with a silent and open expectancy. Our quiet openness allows room for what we seek to reveal itself. We are informed and infused with love and light: informed as knowledge and wisdom forms itself within us, infused as a gentle and energetic radiance permeates our beings.

NO CLINGING

95

*Jesus said,
"If you have money, don't lend it at interest,
but give it to someone who won't give it back to you."*

Security does not exist in this world. Piling up money—all the strenuous efforts to use money to make money—remind me of the hungry ghosts with long narrow skinny throats connecting a gaping cavernous mouth with bloated, perpetually dissatisfied bellies. No matter how much is shoveled in the mouths, the bellies cannot be appeased.

Paradoxically, security does not come from grasping and clinging. Security comes from giving everything away. Continuously. No clinging! We are not talking about just the electronic blips in our accounts nor those tough pieces of paper with no nutritional value. We are talking about an attitude of our hearts.

We are talking about our gifts, the talents we have been given (no charge), which we give to others in turn. Like free-flowing rivers of pure energy, we give our gifts away, expecting nothing in return. Otherwise, we become in-turned ponds of stagnation.

Freely we receive and freely give.

THE TRANSFORMATION OF THE BASE

96
*Jesus said,
"The Kingdom of the Father is like a woman.
She took a little leaven,
concealed it in some dough,
and made it into large loaves of bread.
Let those who have ears hear."*

What is this Kingdom of the Father to which Jesus often refers? Here it is an action, a purposeful action that takes something small, yet containing great possibility, and places it within an element that will not only accept it but will allow itself to be transformed by it into a substance of great nutritional value. Is this not an alchemical process, a procedure transforming lead (inert matter) into gold (radiant vibrancy)?

The Kingdom of the Father is the ongoing transformation of what seems base and useless into that which "feeds the multitudes," whose reverberations expand, providing life beyond itself in a positive and radiant fashion.

The yeast or leaven is available. So is the bread. What is needed is action: the combination of the two. If we have spiritual ears, we can hear this. And by taking action, we allow the action to take place within ourselves.

NO HANDLE

97

Jesus said,
"The Kingdom of the Father is like a woman
who was carrying a jar full of grain.
While she was walking along the road,
still some distance from home,
the handle of the jar broke off
and the grain trickled out behind her on the road.
She didn't realize what was happening.
When she reached her house,
she set the jar down
and found it empty."

Think of the Cosmos being born and flourishing (fleur-ishing, flowering), continuing on its ever-expanding way. Then run the video backward. It is sucked back into emptiness, into the realm of kenosis, into the no-sphere of the Grand Empt, the Kingdom of the Father. (Etymologically speaking, the word "empty" in more than one language comes from root words that meant "freedom," "at leisure.")

The jar is full of grain (our current expansiveness). We are headed for home (the eternal return to our Source). We think we have a handle on it, but we don't. The only way to reach "home" is to let all our accumulation trickle out.

When we finally arrive in the house (of the Father), we put the jar down and find it empty. We laugh great laughter. In that laugh, the jar-carrier and the Father merge as one. We are free.

This is what the Kingdom of the Father is like.

KILLING A POWERFUL MAN

98
Jesus said,
"The Kingdom of the Father is like a man
who wanted to kill a powerful man.
He drew his sword in his own house
and stuck it into the wall,
in order to find out whether his hand
could carry out his intention.
Then he killed the powerful man."

Jesus hangs out with a tough crowd. Some of them want to overthrow the oppressive government. I envision him speaking to a would-be assassin here. His comment is apparently an effective one, since it was saved and repeated.

Jesus knows that the person to whom he's speaking is planning to kill a powerful man. He says, "If you are going to do this, first use the sword in your own house." Do unto yourself what you would do to others. Test your strength.

The wall to stab is the wall of our own limitations, the limits of our tolerance, the boundaries of our worldview. Do any of us have the strength to stab that wall? If we do, then we can go "kill the powerful man." Yet if we do, the need to kill dissolves. Our tolerance no longer has limits. The walls of our worldview expand.

The powerful man who is killed is the one who is holding the sword.

STANDING OUTSIDE

99

His disciples told him,
"Your brothers and your mother are
standing outside."
He said to them,
"These here who do the will of my Father
are my brothers and my mother.
They are the ones
who will enter the Kingdom of my Father."

Your brothers and your mother are standing outside. Already we see a distinction, a barrier. Jesus' earthly kin will not come into the place where he is. After all the fanfare of his birth, his mother may have thought he would be a great rabbi within the Temple, but here he is, on a different course, wandering the streets and visiting in the homes of the riff-raff, the scum, the societal outcasts.

They stand outside. When told they are out there, Jesus does not rush out to greet them. Instead, he strengthens the understanding of the distinction: *These here who do the will of my Father are my brothers and my mother.*

Earthly bonds of kinship give way to spiritual soul links. All who live in accord with the Father—the Source, the One-Who-Breathes-Us—are spiritual kin. We are the ones who will enter the Kingdom. Indeed, we are already in the Kingdom, which is present even now.

THE
THREE

100
They showed Jesus a gold coin and said,
"Caesar's men demand taxes from us."
He answered them,
"Give to Caesar what belongs to Caesar.
Give God what belongs to God.
And give me what is mine."

"They" (perhaps his disciples, perhaps other folk) are under pressure to pay taxes to the ruling power. They do not wish to acknowledge this authority nor give in to it. They come to Jesus, hoping he will resolve their quandary.

Jesus divides the Cosmos neatly into three realms: the realm of the world (*samsara*, in Buddhist terminology), the realm of the divine (*nirvana*), and the realm of individual consciousness. Since his own consciousness is advanced, Jesus knows that samsara is nirvana and nirvana is samsara. He knows that both the world and the divine exist within his own consciousness. The three are one. Yet they are separate.

He says to give the world what is the world's (not what is God's or his), to give God what is God's (not what is the world's or his), and to give him what is his (not what is God's or the world's). To confuse the three is to do violence to all of them.

We exist in the world, but we are not of the world, not spawned by the world. We honor samsara and give it its due. We are aware of the Mystery (God), the Wellspring, That-Which-Breathes-Us. We honor nirvana and release to it what belongs to it. We are aware that we are the gateway between the world and the divine, between samsara and nirvana, and that we embody all three. We delight in what is ours in this perichoretic dance of mutual and reciprocal life.

CONSCIOUSNESS DISCIPLINE

101a
Jesus said,
"Whoever doesn't hate father and mother as I do
cannot become a disciple of mine.
And anyone who doesn't love
father and mother as I do
cannot become a disciple of mine."

We are on a perpetual journey, moving out of that which births us. We must "hate" (turn away from) our past. "No one who puts his hand to the plow and looks back is fit for the kingdom of God" (Luke 9:62). If we are forever looking back, we are continuing to cast ourselves in the same old pillar-of-salt mold.

Yet at the same time, we must "love" (turn toward) our Source and Origin. Turning away from our Source and gazing out into the Void of Becoming while turning toward our Source and receiving encouragement and sustenance: such is the paradox of the spiritual path. This makes us a true disciple (one following the consciousness discipline) of Jesus.

MY MOTHER

101b
*"For my mother . . .
but true she gave me life."*

The incompleteness of this saying leads us to focus on its last six words. "But" is a word used to negate or deflate all that came before and place attention on the primary thought of the sentence.

Whatever my mother has done or not done, has become or is becoming, whatever properties or qualities she has, she has been "true in giving me life."

Jesus is honoring his mother here. Without her willingness to bear him in her womb, he would have no life.

So may we all cherish our mothers despite any disputes.

DOZING DOGS

102
Jesus said,
"Woe to the Pharisees.
They are like a dog
sleeping in the cattle's food trough.
They neither eat nor let the cattle eat."

Jesus is not one to mince words. "Dogs!" he says. Dogs that won't eat and won't let others eat. Sleepers atop spiritual food. Self-appointed guardians of conventionality. Thought police. Guardians of a stagnant tradition. Enforcers of the establishment. Dogs!

The Pharisees lived in ordinary consciousness; they were ordinal and linear in their thoughts, had no spiritual discernment, and were full of themselves. Their minds were made up like a bed in the morning. They did not want any new ideas sliding beneath the covers.

As kids, my siblings and I would sometimes accuse each other of slumbering in our sleep, and then erupt in great peals of laughter. But pharisaical slumber is no laughing matter. As Jesus points out, it is a state calling for woe, intense grief. No one gets fed: neither those of us who are sleeping like dogs nor anyone else, if we can help it.

Anyone who acts like this is a Pharisee. We get caught up in the ten thousand things rather than opening to the flow of the Tao, the Life Force, Spirit. We are in the trance of our stance. We cannot dance the dance. And we want no one else dancing either. Don't they know that life is serious, even grim? By god, we are ready to lay down the law!

NOWHERE FOR THE TIGER TO LAND ITS CLAWS

103
Jesus said,
"Blessed are those
who know where bandits will attack,
so they may get up,
gather their forces,
and arm themselves before the invasion."

Practical common sense, Jesus! What's the big deal here? Even the Boy Scouts know: "Be Prepared!" Our own nation's Homeland Security works on knowing the bandits' movements around the clock.

As always, Jesus has a deeper meaning in mind. He likes to use practical matters to point to spiritual necessities.

The prophets of old said it is the little foxes that eat the grapes. Tai chi wisdom agrees, with the hard-earned understanding that a feather's weight can move a thousand pounds.

The spiritual bandits are small but powerful. They are those parts of ourselves that will come in and throw our well-meaning intentions to the ground and stomp them into the dirt.

We already know what takes us down. We may resist at first, but then we join in with willing cooperation. At its first appearance in our minds, we only catch a whiff of it. A stray thought. A feeling. This is the beginning of the attack. This is the exact time to call upon our assembled forces. This is the time to strike, to move in a way that wards off and renders helpless our spiritual bandit gang.

What are our forces? A strong and centering presence, an open heart of compassion, an ability to focus attention with unbending intent. The three amigos: the immovable stone, the radiant light, and the sword. Season the three with a sense of humor and nothing can stand before us. All bandits gone.

As the Old Dude says in the Tao Te Ching, when we are in tune with our spiritual awareness, "There is nowhere for the rhinoceros to pitch its horn; there is nowhere for the tiger to land its claws; there is nowhere for the weapon to lodge its blade. Why is this so? Because there are no fatal spots on us."

THE BRIDAL CHAMBER

104
They said to Jesus,
"Come, let's pray today. Let's fast."
Jesus replied,
"What sin have I committed?
How have I been overcome?
When the groom leaves the bridal chamber,
then let folk fast and pray."

The bridal chamber is the heart, the heart-mind, the core of our being.

The groom is the radiant presence of our Source.

When the radiant presence of our Source leaves our heart, we should by all means fast and pray, directing full attention to our longing for the groom, for the return of this loving grace in our heart.

Jesus did not need to fast and pray. The radiance was shining steadily at his core.

HIS FATHER
AND
HIS MOTHER

105
Jesus said,
"One who knows his father and his mother
will be called the son of a whore."

Jesus knew from whence he came. The consciousness he embodies is born of the penetrating and the receptive. He is very much aware of his Origin and speaks of it with familiarity (family-arity).

His father and his mother are within him. He is at times more one than the other in his reactions and responses to those around him. He can be like a keen sword or a warm and comforting heart.

Those religious leaders caught in ordinary consciousness thought him a heretic: a teacher and follower of false doctrine, one who had gone whoring away from "the true religion." Ordinary consciousness cannot comprehend spiritual consciousness. The world cannot understand that in which it is embedded.

MAKING THE TWO INTO ONE

106
Jesus said,
"When you make the two one,
you will become the sons of men.
When you say, 'Move, mountain!'
it will move."

Jesus speaks of *men and sons of men* (gender does not play a part here; the reference is to all humanity). "Men" refers to the consciousness state that has existed on earth for some time, the consciousness state of duality: this versus that, self versus other, us versus our Source. "Sons of men" refers to the consciousness state of future humanity, a consciousness that is roaming the earth right now in some folk, the consciousness state Jesus embodied: no separation, the consciousness state of the non-dual.

When you make the two one, you will become the sons of men. When we open to a non-dual state of consciousness, we are in the ranks of future humanity. We are opening to the evolution of human consciousness.

As we do so, all things are possible. *When you say, "Move, mountain!" it will move.* This does not mean that we shall be shifting mountain ranges here and there all over the place. It means that when we face an obstacle, we can command it to move out of the way.

We will have and are developing even now the skillful means (*upaya*, as the Mahayana Buddhists say) to transform our world—both our individual world and our societal world, for those two shall also be made into one.

OUTSIDE THE CAMP

107
Jesus said,
"The Kingdom is like a shepherd
with a hundred sheep.
One of them, the largest, went astray.
He left the ninety-nine sheep
and went looking for that one
until he found it.
When he had gone to such trouble,
he said to the sheep,
'I love you more than the ninety-nine.'"

Awareness does not want to lose any of its awareness-ing. Especially a large awareness-ing that has wandered off and lost contact. All the other awarenesses will be left behind, snug in their fold, never venturing out. The Awareness that encompasses all will seek the venturer, the one who wandered off, will seek to the point of exhaustion. In doing so, Awareness Itself is changed. It says: "I love you more than the ones who stay within the fold."

RESONANCE

108
*Jesus said,
"The person who drinks from my mouth
will become like me.
I will become that person,
and the hidden things
will be revealed to that person."*

The gift of Vision, the opening of the third eye (our first two eyes being the sensory and the intellectual), arrives and is cultivated by the process of resonance.

One meaning of *resonate* is "to vibrate in harmony with." When one string is plucked on a well-tuned violin, the other strings vibrate in harmony. When our awareness is attuned to the awareness embodied and inspirited by Jesus, our awareness opens to Jesus' awareness. We vibrate with his consciousness.

The principle producing this phenomenon is commonplace: Whatever we attend to, we become. When we attend to the desire of our genitals, we become walking sex organs.

When we attend to our loving open hearts, we become compassion on earth. When we attend to anger, fear, and hatred, we become war machines. And so on. Whatever we attend to, we become.

This is why meditation, prayer, and contemplation are so important. We reserve time daily to attend to higher, wider, and deeper realms. We become more resonant with those realms. This is a process of co-creation. We have to do our part. The universe (the bubbling spring) does the rest.

Whatever we attend to, we become.

Jesus is saying that if we attend to what he is embodying and in-spiriting (if we drink from his mouth), we will become like him—and even more powerfully, Jesus will become us. As that happens—as we allow that to happen—what was mysterious becomes clear. Christ consciousness (Cosmic awareness) and our consciousness become one.

A
TREASURE

109
Jesus said,
"The Kingdom is like a man
who had a hidden treasure in his
field without knowing it.
He died and left the field to his son.
The son knew nothing about the treasure,
and, having inherited the field, sold it.
While plowing the field, the one who bought it
found the treasure.
He began to lend money at interest
to anyone he wished."

The Kingdom (which is spread out on the earth but no one sees it) is like the man with a treasure of which he is unaware hidden in his field.

The Kingdom is *not* like the son in the parable nor is it like the new owner, both of whom made money from the field (the son selling his life away, ignorant of the treasure he contained; the new owner very much aware of the spiritual domain, controlling who had access to it and requiring interest payments).

The Kingdom is like the man who died and never knew it was there. We have a treasure hidden in the fields of energy that we are. The Kingdom is within us. We are the temple of God. But if we're not careful, we may die and not know—not act upon, not live by—this deep-core treasure.

LETTING GO

110
Jesus said,
"Whoever finds the world
and becomes rich
should renounce the world."

We spend the first part of our lives trying to find the world. We want to know our place in it. We want to belong. We want to contribute. We amass stuff.

We spend the second part of our lives letting go. We let go of stuff. We let go of social roles. We let go of others' definitions of us and of our set-in-concrete definitions of ourselves. We understand the value of not clinging. Our richness is now in our simplicity, in our nothingness.

ROLL UP

111a
Jesus said,
"The earth and the sky
will be rolled up right in front of you.
Anyone living from the Living One
will not see death."

Take no time to stare at the idols we have created as our brave new world. We are moving into a new consciousness structure, one that's diaphanous, transparent, open.

We are moving into the consciousness structure Jesus speaks of here. *The earth and sky will be rolled up right in front of you.* First, the earth and the sky roll up right in front of us, confronting us, staring deeply into our souls. Then they roll up like a projection screen or a window shade. All falls away around us, infinity in every direction.

There is nothing to be frightened of here. Awestruck, yes, but not fearful. *Anyone living from the Living One will not see death.*

What is this undying living from which we live? That which breathes us. That which gives us life. We are the Source sourcing. We are the Source embodying. This is the consciousness structure to which we open ourselves. This is who we are.

We walk the planet as universal beings. All is transformed. All is transforming.

UNCONTAINABLE

111b
Doesn't Jesus say,
"The world is not worthy
of those who have found themselves"?

When we know who we are, the human-created society of socio-political games cannot contain us. We move beyond all bounds, outside all camps, able to warm ourselves at every campfire but attached to none. We are the Tao taoing, God godding, the Buddha on his buddha cycle.

We are the gleams in a lover's eye, the spontaneous laughter of joyous children, the silent unfolding of unseen flowers. The world is lint within our navels, monkey piss on Buddha's finger, leftover news on the pressroom floor.

Gate, gate, paragate, says the Heart Sutra: Gone! Gone! Gone beyond Gone, utterly Gone!

THE SOUL-AND-FLESH TANGO

112
Jesus said,
"Woe to the flesh that's depending on the soul.
Woe to the soul depending on the flesh."

"Woe is me for I am undone," said the prophet (Isaiah 6:5). Woe is a state of complete unraveling. The center does not hold: utter complete devastation. If you have not been in that state, you are not completely human. As the Sufi chef said to the chickpea trying to climb out of the pot, "Get back in there, you're not done yet."

We are souls immersed in flesh, embryos of God firmly planted in the ground of existence, embodyings of the Great Mystery. As such, we are subject to great woe, victims of a double jeopardy. Woe to the flesh that depends on the soul, for the flesh will surely get crucified as it follows the lead of the soul. Woe to the soul that depends on the flesh, for the soul becomes an angel of tarnished dirt and ripped, useless wings.

What to do? Merge. Claim my merge-inity. Become a merge-ion. Let the flesh become an extension of the soul. Allow the soul to radiate outward as one expression. The embryo loves its womb. And in a very real sense the embryo *is* its womb at this time. The embryo and the womb become as one. The soul and flesh tango.

THE KINGDOM

113
His disciples asked him,
"When is the Kingdom coming?"
Jesus replied,
"It won't come by waiting for it.
It won't be a matter of saying,
'Here it is,' or 'There it is.'
Rather, the Kingdom of the Father
is already spread out on the earth,
and people don't see it."

What we are looking for—the Kingdom of the Father, Home—is already here. It is our awareness that falls short. We become so engrossed in our meat-ness and its desires and irritations, so pumped up in our social roles, that we become blind, insensitive. We think we are going somewhere . . . when we have already arrived.

Those who point to a future arrival of the Kingdom are magicians of misdirection. Now is the future, and it contains all time, all space. *The Kingdom of the Father is already spread out on the earth, and people don't see it.*

We are concentric spheres of awareness. We sit in the seats at the centers of our souls. We open to the Cosmos, the playground and the Kingdom of our source. We are always already in the Kingdom.

SIMON PETER SAID

114

Simon Peter said to them,
"Let Mary leave us
because women are not worthy of life."
Jesus answered,
"Look, I myself shall lead her
in order to make her male,
so that she can become a living spirit,
resembling you males.
For every woman who makes herself male
will enter into the Kingdom of Heaven."

This saying appears to have been tacked on to the Gospel of Thomas. Not only is it inconsistent with the tone of Jesus' earlier sayings (especially saying 22), it starts out with "Simon Peter said." This advocacy of male supremacy became a cornerstone of the institutional church's dogma, and it has helped lead to its weakening and downfall. The appropriate ending of the Gospel of Thomas is Saying 113. Nevertheless, I will provide a commentary:

Some men have trouble accepting the feminine parts of themselves. They want to drive away the feminine, saying it is not worthy. They like hard-core, slam-dunk masculinity and regard the open, compassionate aspects of themselves as weakness. That adamant maleness irrupts here in Peter's words.

Each of us is an interflow of male and female energies. When we recognize that, when we allow that, we enter into a state of higher consciousness, of greater awareness. We have transcended gender. We have, as Jesus said in saying 22, made "the male and the female the same, so that the male isn't male and the female isn't female."

AFTERWORD

Some decades ago, the words from Habakkuk 2:2—to "write the vision and make it plain so that those who run may read and that those who read may run"—pierced my soul—my heart-mind—as a strong command.

I sincerely pray that this commentary is in accord with that instruction. As you run busily through life, may you find time to read these sayings of Jesus and take them to heart. May you find energy in these sayings and in the commentary, causing you to run more freely and joyously.

If you have ears, you will hear. If you hear something richer and deeper than what I heard, my goal will have been accomplished.

Selah and Amen.
—*George Breed*

ABOUT THE AUTHOR

George Breed is a teacher of spiritual dynamics, has a doctorate in psychology, and is the author of several books: *The Inner Work of the Warrior: Embodying Spirit* (available from Anamchara Books), *Zen Baptist: Sunday Sermons and Weekday Sutras from a Lover of Jesus and Student of Buddha* (also available from Anamchara Books), *Silence Whispers*, *Radical Openness*, *The Adventures of Stagger Li*, and the co-author of *The World's First Ever Baptist Crime Novel*. A sampling of his many presentations at local, state, national, and international professional conferences include *Application of Martial Art Principles to Daily Life*; *Work as the Practice of Joy*; *Radical Spirituality: Sacredly Engaging the Profane*; *The Use of Mind and Spirit in Healing*; *The Caduceus as Model for Nonverbal Communicative Styles*; *Centering: A Return to the Temple*. George lives at the base of a currently dormant volcano in northern Arizona with his partner, Karen, and the warrior cat, Kato.

CHECK OUT THIS OTHER TITLE FROM

George Breed

Zen Baptist: Sunday Sermons & Weekday Sutras from a Lover of Jesus & Student of Buddha

Author: George Breed
Price: $14.95
Paperback
ISBN: 978-1-937211-70-7

I am a Zen Baptist—a peculiar sort of Baptist to be sure. Buddhists of old were horrified by Zen Buddhists chopping up wooden likenesses of the Buddha for firewood. This Zen Baptist has no problem with chopping up images of Jesus which have become wooden and restrictive over the years, stumbling blocks. Of course, some will be horrified. It matters not. Jesus understands.
 —George Breed

Here's an example of one of George's Sunday sermons:

Turn in your Bibles to Isaiah 6:5: "Woe is me! for I am undone."

Have you ever had your life put together so nicely, running along smoothly, everything just humming, and then—blam!—it all falls or flies apart, blown into smithereens? There you are, left sitting in the ashes of the aftermath, wondering what the hell and why in heaven's name.

Congratulations, you have just become undone.

But life has its rhythms. For things to fall together, they usually have to fall apart first.

Sometimes we need some woe—some whoa!—in order to smash our assumptions. Otherwise we get too certain, too smug, too absolutely sure we know what's what. When we get that way, the universe in its wonderfulness allows us to become undone. A fresh start opens.

Zen teaches that emptiness is a creative place to be. The ancient Chinese referred to the zone of emptiness out of which all arises as "wu" or "wu chi." The Japanese call it "ku." I like to call it the "wu chi ku" . . . and when we are in the undone place, we can all dance the wu chi ku.

Please stand up and turn to page 148, the song of the undone: "Just As I Am, Without One Plea."

CHECK OUT THIS OTHER TITLE FROM

George Breed

The Inner Work of the Warrior: Embodying Spirit
Author: George Breed
Price: $14.95
Paperback
ISBN: 978-1-937211-90-5

Warriors of spirit across the ages and across disciplines (martial arts, healing arts, creative arts, spiritual arts, political arts) embody certain qualities. In embodying (deeply practicing) these qualities, stress effects are reduced, increased energy results, awareness expands, confidence deepens, the mind grows quiet and more open to creative solutions, right relationships occurs, and the state known as "flow" becomes one's lifestyle. The embodying of these qualities is an essential next step in the transformation of human consciousness and in the survival of the human species.

You are invited to include these qualities on your journey, to sit with them, entertain them, try them on for size . . . and perhaps find they become you.

Brother Lawrence: A Christian Zen Master

Author: Brother Lawrence
Price: $12.95
Paperback
114 pages
ISBN: 978-1-933630-97-7

Brother Lawrence's famous work, The Practice of the Presence of God, is broken into bite-size pieces and paired with the writings of some of the greatest Zen teachers, from the Buddha to the Dalai Lama. The result sheds new light on this great Christian classic, offering profoundly practical insights for the spiritual life.

"You could read this book in an hour, but take the rest of your life to absorb its wisdom. It will help you 'become a master of your own bliss, a chemist of your own joy.' In a time when religious misunderstanding abounds, this book is a bridge between traditions. I wish every Christian would read, mark, learn, and inwardly digest the teaching of Brother Lawrence, Christian Zen Master, here illuminated by the richness of Buddhist texts."
—the Rev. Mark Giroux, Rector, St. Mark's Episcopal Church, Chenango Bridge, New York; Member of the Children of Abraham (a continuing interfaith conversation of Jews, Christians, and Muslims); Member of the Broome County Interfaith Clergy Collective

Anamchara Books
Books to Inspire
Your Spiritual Journey

In Celtic Christianity, an *anamchara* is a soul friend, a companion and mentor (often across the miles and the years) on the spiritual journey. Soul friendship entails a commitment to both accept and challenge, to reach across all divisions in a search for the wisdom and truth at the heart of our lives.

At Anamchara Books, we are committed to creating a community of soul friends by publishing books that lead us into deeper relationships with God, the Earth, and each other. These books connect us with the great mystics of the past, as well as with more modern spiritual thinkers. They are designed to build bridges, shaping an inclusive spirituality where we all can grow.

You can order our books at **www.AnamcharaBooks.com**. Check out our site to read opinions and perspectives from our editorial staff on our Soul Friends blog. You can also submit your own blog posts by emailing **info@AnamcharaBooks.com** with "Blog Entry for Soul Friends" in the subject line. To find out more about Anamchara Books and connect with others on their own spiritual journeys, visit **www.AnamcharaBooks.com** today.

Anamchara Books
220 Front Street
Vestal, New York 13850
(607) 785-1578
www.AnamcharaBooks.com

www.ingramcontent.com/pod-product-compliance
Lightning Source LLC
Chambersburg PA
CBHW060517080526
44586CB00012B/512